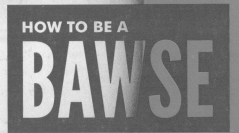

HOW TO BE A
BAWSE

HOW

BA

A GUIDE TO

LILLY

TO BE A

WISE

BALLANTINE BOOKS
NEW YORK

~~SURVIVING~~ ING LIFE
CONQUERING

SINGH

PENGUIN RANDOM HOUSE

UK | USA | Canada | Ireland | Australia
India | New Zealand | South Africa

First published in the United States of America by Ballantine Books,
an imprint of Random House, a division of Penguin Random House LLC, New York 2017
First published in Great Britain by Penguin Random House UK, 2017
007

Part-title illustrations by Ed Harrington
All photos, unless indicated otherwise, are by Danielle Levitt

Remaining photo credits are located on p. 318

Book design by Laura Palese

Printed in India by Replika Press Pvt. Ltd.

A CIP catalogue record for this book is available from the British Library

HARDBACK ISBN: 978-0-718-18553-4
TRADE PAPERBACK: 978-0-718-18691-3

www.greenpenguin.co.uk

DEDICATED TO

THE PERSON I WAS

SIX YEARS AGO.

I TOLD YOU TO

KEEP
GOING.

THANKS FOR LISTENING.

PART 3
MAKE HEADS TURN

PART 4
BE A UNICORN

HOLY CRAP, I WROTE A BOOK!

Wait. Let me back up here. Hi! My name is **LILLY** . . .
and **HOLY CRAP,** I wrote a book!
If you're reading this, I'm assuming
it's for one of **THREE** reasons:

YOU ARE FAMILIAR WITH MY YOUTUBE VIDEOS and also know me as Superwoman. If so, thanks for supporting me outside of the digital space and allowing me to come through your screen and into your home like that terrifying lady from *The Ring*. Come to think of it, we have similar hair, so I apologize in advance for that terribly accurate comparison. **Seven days** JK! I'm chill.

YOU'RE A PARENT AND FOUND THIS in your child's bedroom and you're curious. You're also nosy and want to ensure that this book isn't filled with filth that will corrupt your baby's brain. Hi there! I can assure you that this book is family-friendly with a healthy hint of sass. My goal is to inspire your baby to work hard and achieve great things. You should definitely buy three more copies and plant them around the house.

YOU HAVE NO IDEA WHO I AM or you've vaguely heard of me. That's completely fine. Maybe you're a total stranger who just wants to know how to be a Bawse, or maybe you are looking to add some diversity into your life.

ODUCTION

Regardless of how you got here, I'm so glad you did. Thank you for spending your valuable time and hard-earned money on this book. For those of you who aren't familiar with me, I'm best known for creating uplifting, comedic videos on YouTube, amongst other things. I'm the holder of a psychology degree, an activist for gender equality, an occasional rapper, a sister, a unicorn, and now an author.

The last few years of my life have been pretty crazy! I've done everything from kissing Seth Rogen while dressed up as my mom to having my face plastered across Times Square to helping send girls in Kenya to school. I always knew I wanted to write a book, but I wanted to wait until I felt like I truly had something to say. I'm not that old or wise, so this is not a memoir. Instead, this book is an accumulation of lessons I've learned that I want to share with you. They are the things that have made me a Bawse. What's a Bawse, you ask? Great question!

A Bawse is like a boss, but so epic that I had to change the spelling. Unlike a boss, who is defined as such only within the workplace, a Bawse is someone who excels in both personal and professional settings. A Bawse exudes confidence, turns heads, gets hurt efficiently, communicates effectively, and hustles relentlessly. My hope is that this book will unleash your inner Bawse and give you the tools necessary to not only survive life but conquer it.

This book is divided into four sections, each filled with chapters that illustrate a specific theme. Within each chapter I relay a lesson I've learned and how you can best apply that lesson to your life. At the end of each section, you'll also see that I've included a feature entitled "Out of the Blue." These sections are very important to me because they describe a time in my life when I was fighting depression and also allow me to highlight a moment from my life post-depression. I included these essays because I think it's important to know who you're taking advice from. I want you to know that I've been through some tough challenges and that the lessons I'm sharing with you in this book were not easily learned. I'm not writing about mythical, fairy-tale stuff. I'm telling you what has actually worked in my life, the things that pulled me out of a place of deep depression into a life filled with the kind of success I couldn't have ever imagined. Let's be real: a billion views on the Internet and millions of subscribers don't justify why you should take advice from me. But hopefully these "Out of the Blue" sections will.

I'm not an expert and I'm not claiming to be one. However, I've had some truly unique experiences that have taught me valuable lessons. I'm writing this book for the same reason I started making YouTube videos: because I want to be a positive light in this world. This book isn't merchandise or a check mark on my to-do list; it's so much more than that. When I was going through my darkest days, the smallest thing could flip a switch in my brain and change my day from horrible to not so bad. You have dreams and goals you want to achieve. We all do. Maybe you're already on a steady path to success, or maybe you're struggling to make ends meet. Either way, I want this book to flip that switch. I want you to accomplish everything you ever wanted in life, and I truly believe you can. But it won't be easy.

Being a Bawse is hard work. It requires an unfathomable amount of dedication and hustle. The following pages do not contain tricks, quick tips, or get-rich-quick schemes. I'm not going to tell you about any short-cuts or good luck charms. Instead, I am going to make your work ethic sweat, your mind expand, your fear dissolve, and your obstacles crumble.

If you're ready to conquer your life, turn the page. It's time to be a Bawse.

I'm rooting for you with all my heart.

Lilly x

THIS BOOK IS NOT A SURVIVAL GUIDE FILLED WITH HOPEFUL THOUGHTS, LUCKY CHARMS, OR FLUFFY QUOTES. THERE WILL BE NO SECRET SCHEMES TO A REWARDING LIFE FOUND IN THESE PAGES. THAT'S BECAUSE SUCCESS, HAPPINESS, AND EVERYTHING ELSE THAT FEELS GREAT IN LIFE HAVE NO ESCALATORS. THERE ARE ONLY STAIRS. THIS BOOK WILL BE YOUR PERSONAL TRAINER, GUIDING YOU UP THOSE STAIRS. START STRETCHING.

RULES

FOR READING

THIS BOOK

←-------------------→

1   **LIKE MOST RULES, EVERY RULE IN THIS BOOK** has an exception. In fact, don't even think of these chapters as rules; think of them as guidelines. Don't look for the unique scenario that disproves my point. In other words, don't be that annoying person in the YouTube comments section who has to be a Debbie Downer. If I say "SMILE!" don't yell, "But what if someone got paralyzed in a bungee-jumping accident and fractured their jaw and doesn't have the ability to smile anymore, Lilly?" Don't focus on finding the loopholes but instead use that energy and focus on what you can learn. Also, if you got into a bungee-jumping accident and only fractured your jaw, you have a lot to smile about!

2   **BEFORE YOU READ THIS BOOK, I NEED YOU** to lay down your defense mechanisms. Take them off and put them away. I'm going to call you out and tell you you're slacking. I'm going to shine a spotlight on issues that make you uncomfortable and that you want to avoid. There's no room for excuses, justifications, or pity parties. Read the chapters with an open mind and resist the urge to get offended or defensive.

THIS BOOK HAS A LOT OF INFORMATION IN IT. I know that because it took me fifty years (an estimation) to write. Don't feel bad if you forget things! In fact, I encourage you to read chapters over and over again because becoming a Bawse is a process that doesn't happen overnight. Take notes. Rip out pages and plaster them to your wall. Do whatever you need to do to retain these guidelines.

 IN A LOT OF THE CHAPTERS, I talk about how I apply each Bawse rule to my life. If you can't relate to these specific scenarios, that's completely fine and understandable. The goal is to understand the general principle and adapt it to your situation. I'm providing you with a framework—it's up to you to tweak it.

 DON'T GET MAD at yourself or feel discouraged. This book is an opportunity to call yourself out, grow, make mistakes, and become better. Reading this book should be viewed as a journey toward something positive, not an exercise in judgment and criticism.

ALL RIGHT, HERE WE GO!

Start stretching! It's about to get real.

*cue *Rocky* theme song*

ARE YOU READY?!

(please proceed to beat your chest with determination)

THIS IS THE MOMENT!

(would be great if you could clench your fists in preparation)

THE TIME IS NOW!

(initiate heavy breathing—bonus points if you squint)

3 . . . *(maybe jump a little)*

2 . . . *(roaring noises are encouraged)*

1 . . .

HERE WE GO!!!! IT'S TIME TO BE A BAWSE.

PART 1
MASTER YOUR MIND

Our mind is our biggest asset, but also our biggest obstacle. It is the most important tool we possess, but it is useless if we don't know how to apply it. In this section you will learn how to befriend your mind, control it, and become more self-aware. Moreover, you'll learn about all the tricks your mind can play on you and how to be the best referee possible. If you want to be a Bawse, your brain needs to get on board.

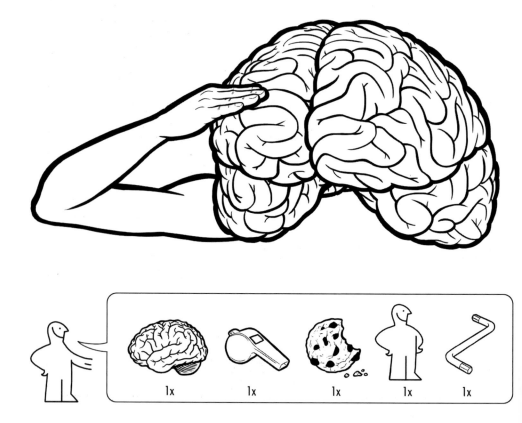

1x   1x   1x   1x   1x

CHAPTER 1

PLAY
NINTENDO

I'M SWEATING

in my blue overalls as I look at all the obstacles ahead of me. I have three options: (1) pound my head on this brick block and hope for a star, (2) run and jump over the enemy, or (3) stomp on this turtle's head and force him to retract into his shell. No matter which option I go with, the fact remains that the Koopa Troopa up ahead is going to stay there. I can't control it or convince it that it's actually a Ninja Turtle and thus is in the wrong game. That's fine. No Ninja Turtles means more pizza for me, and I'm Italian, so this is all working out. I know the Koopa Troopa isn't going to listen to me, and therefore I need to control the only thing I can—and that's me, Mario.

Videogames are a great analogy for life. You go through levels, get thrown off by obstacles, and face several enemies. The game will become harder and harder, but it's okay because you become smarter, faster, and more skilled. When playing a videogame, you control a character by making it jump, run, duck, and attack. I mean, that was back in my day when my Super Nintendo controller had two buttons. Today videogame controllers have as many buttons as a keyboard, so who knows what you can do. You can probably press $A + Y + Z$ while twirling your left joystick and your character will sing the national anthem. Either way, the fact remains that your character is the only thing you can control in the game. The enemies will keep coming, the walls will keep shrinking, and the time will keep ticking away. It's your job to navigate your character through a situation you cannot control.

That's exactly how you should view life. A Bawse understands that there are many things in life you have no control over and it is inefficient to become frustrated by that reality. Not being able to control people and situations doesn't make you powerless; it just means you have to exercise your power in a different way. If you can't control people, then control your reaction to them. If you can't control a situation, then prepare for it.

Before I started my career in the entertainment industry, I was the leader of a small dance company (if you could even call it that) in Toronto. We started off small, with only a few dancers, specializing in only Indian dance styles, but over time, in true Lilly fashion, I wanted to keep growing and expanding our horizons. Since I was little I've had larger-than-life ideas. I never wanted to settle for something simple or mediocre, and as a result, when I did things, I wanted them to be the biggest and best things. There were so many other dance teams and companies around and I didn't want to just be another addition to an already long list. I committed my days to transforming the company in the hopes of creating a dance empire that would take over the world. I really thought that was possible. We would be dancing Power Rangers who saved the world, one extended leg and pointed toe at a time. I decided to convert my basement into a full-blown office. We held auditions for dancers who were skilled in all forms of dance so that we could perform hip-hop, classical, and fusion in addition to what we were already doing. I organized photo shoots and video shoots and other creative marketing techniques. I had so much drive and determination that no injury, financial strain, or competition could steer me off my path. What I couldn't see, however, was the one obstacle that was in front of me the entire time, and which caused everything to fall apart: the team itself.

I had such big dreams for the company and I was always willing to work for them. Without hesitation, I would pull all-nighters to put together marketing materials, spend money out of my own pocket to invest in what we needed, and drive myself crazy thinking of innovative ways to set ourselves apart. But then I would arrive at practice and deal with three dancers showing up late, one

66 IF YOU CAN'T CONTROL PEOPLE, THEN CONTROL YOUR REACTION TO THEM. IF YOU CAN'T CONTROL A SITUATION, THEN PREPARE FOR IT.

not showing up at all, and two of them leaving early. Getting people to put in work on events to help our brand was like pulling teeth. We often performed at weddings and thus needed to adhere to a professional dress code, yet some dancers would occasionally show up wearing shorts and flip-flops. I would get so frustrated with them because I was putting in

"

VIDEOGAMES ARE A GREAT ANALOGY **FOR LIFE. YOU GO THROUGH** LEVELS, **GET THROWN OFF BY** OBSTACLES, **AND FACE** SEVERAL ENEMIES.

"

so much work for this dream, but the reality of the situation was that the dream was mine, not theirs. I tried for years to control them and make them work for something they didn't care about as much as I did, and it just didn't work.

My dance company dreams faded away gradually, but the process was hastened by my discovery of YouTube. I remember feeling a new sensation the first time I uploaded a video. I wrote the script, shot it, edited it, and released it. No one else was involved or required, and the independence was exhilarating. Soon I developed an even greater drive and passion for my career as Superwoman than I'd had previously with my dance team. This time, however, I wasn't trying to control a group of twenty people every time I needed something to get done. The only person I needed to control was the only person I could control, and that was me.

Today, of course, I have a team that surrounds me and helps me to build my business. But Lilly is still at the root of Superwoman. The success of Superwoman and the failure of my dance team helped me learn a very important lesson: work with what's in your control. This lesson can be applied to so many situations in our lives. You get frustrated when your parents nag you, so every time they do, you storm out of the room. You can't control your parents, so stop trying. Instead, use that energy to control your reaction the next time they nag you. You might not be able to smash a brick block and find a star that makes you invincible, but you can practice patience and build up a resistance to nagging. If none of that works, you can find the closest green tube and transport yourself out of the conversation.

Have you ever played a videogame, then lost because you realized you were looking at the wrong part of the screen the whole time? You were so confused as to why your controller wasn't working, but really you were just trying to control the wrong character. That's what trying to control people is like in real life. We're so often fixated on getting people to behave in accordance with what we want that we forget to focus on ourselves.

The best way to stop people from pushing your buttons is to start pushing your own.

A + Y + Z. Left joystick.

"O Canada."

CHAPTER 2

CONQUER

YOUR

THOUGHTS

<----------------->

TOUCH YOUR NOSE.

No, I'm serious. I want you to stop reading after this sentence and don't resume until you take your right hand and use it to touch the tip of your nose.

Do it.

Look at you! What an impressive piece of machinery you are. Do you know what you just did? You were introduced to a thought and decided to act on it; your brain sent signals using neurotransmitters, through neurons, across your body, and into your arm, prompting it to move and touch your magnificent nose.

Why did I just make you touch your nose? Because I'm Simon and I run this town! No, but really, it was to show you that YOU control your mind; your mind doesn't control you. You successfully directed your brain to touch your nose. Understanding your mind's power is key to being a Bawse. Imagine using that same type of direction to instruct your mind to stop being negative, or jealous, or terrified. We often feel that we are slaves to biology. People say things like "I just can't help but feel that way" or "I can't control being jealous." But I believe that, in most situations, we can teach our minds to function with more positivity and efficiency. In other words, by understanding that mushy sponge in our skulls, we can conquer our thoughts.

What does conquering your thoughts mean? First, it means you get to wear an awesome warrior costume, so congrats on that victory! #OOTD Also, it means understanding why you feel the way you feel, what prompts you to carry out certain actions, what causes specific reactions, and what circumstances lead you to make regrettable decisions. Once you discover all the ins and outs of your mind, you basically have the cheat code to your game of life. All you have to do is input the data and you have access to extra mental weapons, stronger protection, and new passageways. Notice I said YOUR game of life and not THE game of life. That's because everyone's mind is different. The cheat codes you discover for your mind cannot be applied to all of humanity. I'm not encouraging you to study the

BIOLOGY of the brain (it is fascinating, but also, who has that much time?). I'm encouraging you to study your specific psychological makeup.

I was forced to learn how to conquer my thoughts because of the nature of my job. For six years I've been posting videos twice a week on the Internet. I have over 500 videos on my main channel and 500 videos on my second channel—that's over 1,000 videos for people around the globe to view and judge as harshly as they desire. The Internet is wonderful and revolutionary, but let's face it, it can also be extremely cruel. People feel they can say anything to you when they are sitting comfortably behind their computer screen being completely anonymous. When I first started posting videos, I got a lot of support (mostly because my friends and family would watch and they felt obligated to be nice. Also, I had a second account that I would use to compliment myself. Oops!), but with time I started to receive negative, hateful comments and I didn't know how to react. Here are a few examples (word for word, without spellcheck) of the comments I've received:

> This lily Singh paki ***** needs to die she's everywhere I hate seeing her Bengali paki face I hope she gets cancer or her mum dies slowly j painfully leave focus tube alone up horrible black *****

> This is why women shouldn't have rights.

> This video gave me cancer

> she is so ****ing stupid. she only get famous because she hot and thst sells but she is still dumb. I hope someone shoots her

FUN!

Do hateful comments still bother me? Sometimes, but not as often. How did I deal with them? When people ask me this, my response is usually, "I developed a thick skin." But what I really mean is, I learned how to conquer my thoughts. This is how I broke it down:

People are leaving mean comments.

Why?
Maybe it's because my videos suck.

Do you say mean things to people when you think they suck?
No. Not unless I'm having a bad day or in a bad mood.

Maybe people leaving the negative comments are having a bad day. Maybe that's what the comment is really about.

But the comments make me feel insecure.

Do you like your videos?

Yes.

So should your opinion of your videos be dependent on what other people think? Is that the type of person you want to be?

Not at all.

So it doesn't make sense to let the negative opinions of others impact what you think.

Maybe I should stop making videos, though.

Does making videos make you happy?

Yes, very.

Do you believe you should value negative comments above your own happiness?

That doesn't sound right. Maybe I should just reply to them?

Or you could spend more time replying to people that make you feel good so they're more encouraged to keep supporting you.

Now, you may think a convo like this sounds a bit naive. OF COURSE people want to be happy and ignore negative comments, but it's easier said than done. That's why it's important to closely analyze this conversation and discover all the cheat codes hidden within it.

1 "Maybe they're having a bad day." CHEAT CODE ONE: Lilly, when people do or say hurtful things to you, there's a chance they may actually be upset about something else in their life.

2 "Should other opinions impact what you think about yourself?" CHEAT CODE TWO: Lilly, sometimes when you hear other opinions you'll feel pressured to change your own. Before you enter into situations in which you will be confronted with a lot of opinions, make sure you strongly believe your own.

3 "I don't want to stop making videos, because they make me happy." CHEAT CODE THREE: Your happiness is stronger than fear. You can continue battling fear as long as your videos make you happy. Make sure you prioritize creating content that makes you happy; otherwise fear and negativity will slowly take over.

4 "Maybe I should reply to them." CHEAT CODE FOUR: Recognize that replying was suggested to make you feel better. Understand this impulse and catch it before you act on it. Make yourself feel better in a more constructive way.

The cheat codes I discovered while dealing with YouTube comments have been useful in so many areas of my life. When someone cuts me off while driving, I apply cheat code one so that I don't overreact: the person driving could be upset about something in their life. Cutting me off wasn't about ME. When a brand offers me a lot of money to make a video I don't actually like, I implement cheat code three: my content has to make me happy, otherwise negativity will start to seep in. When I'm having an argument and want to make an unnecessary remark to get the last word in, I try to catch myself because I know I'm just trying to make myself feel better—thus cheat code four. If I've gotten myself into an upsetting situation, it's usually because I ignored a cheat code or pattern in my behavior.

Conquering your thoughts is not a task that can be accomplished overnight, or over many nights, to be honest. It's an ongoing process that requires frequent readjustment because your mind is constantly evolving. It requires you to ask yourself a lot of questions and to analyze the answers honestly. From now on start asking yourself WHY you feel a certain way, WHAT made you perform a certain action, and HOW you could do things differently. The information you discover is powerful because it helps you to discover patterns and in turn use your mind productively and efficiently. After all, your mind is your most powerful tool, but it's not useful if you don't know how to use it. It's like trying to fix a printer with a stapler: it doesn't work. Trust me, I've tried.

The key is to use a hammer because all printers suck.

CHAPTER 3

BE

ECRETIVE

MY MOM ONCE TOLD ME,

"The more details people know about you, the weaker you become." These words of wisdom came between "What did I do to deserve these crazy children?" and "You still haven't put music on my iPod." And I've come to learn that she was right. At first I thought she was being cynical. In my mind, her words translated as "Don't trust anyone." But over time, I learned there is a difference between trusting people and allowing yourself to be too vulnerable. Sometimes it is nice and necessary to feel a little vulnerable in relationships, but I don't believe anyone should know *everything* about you. As long as you're self-aware, it's okay to keep some of your strengths and weaknesses a secret.

Now, hold on! Do you hear that? It's the sound of people getting ready to defend their relationships. Please stop. I don't have a bartender serving me unlimited cosmos to sit through this right now. (Also, why don't I? Note to self: hire bartender.) A healthy relationship, of any kind, doesn't require telling someone every single detail about yourself. Hear me out.

It was another wise mother, like my own, who showed me how powerful the use of selective secrecy can be: Daenerys Targaryen, Mother of Dragons, first of her name, breaker of chains, and Woman Crush Wednesday of millions. Now, if you've never watched *Game of Thrones,* first of all, you should be absolutely ashamed of your ridiculous priorities thus far in life, and second of all, if you plan to start watching it, skip ahead a little bit because—

SPOILER ALERT! You've been warned.

—everyone dies.

Just kidding.

But am I?

As I'm writing this, season 6 just came to an end, so let's focus on what's happened thus far, and hopefully by the time this book comes out, I won't be eating my words. (Apparently it takes more than a few days to publish a book. WEIRD.) In short, everything seems to be working in favor of Daenerys. She has a large army, a loyal following, three dragons (yes, that's a thing), and great hair. She's on her way to conquer the Seven Kingdoms (basically, the world), and there is very little standing in her way. In fact, I often hear fans talk about how "lucky" Daenerys is because solutions just seem to fall into her lap. It is at this point that I stop the entire conversation, turn off the lights, start up my PowerPoint presentation, and thoroughly explain why Daenerys isn't lucky—she's just super-smart and understands the power of being secretive.

(It would be great if you could also turn off the lights and read this with a lamp for dramatic effect. I'll wait . . .)

. . .

. . .

SEASON 1, EPISODE 1! We are first introduced to Daenerys in a scene where her brother speaks down to her in a disrespectful manner and she says nothing to defend herself. She just listens to him obediently and therefore leaves the viewer to assume she is weak, impressionable, and easily taken advantage of. Before this emotional scene ends, something very important yet very minor happens. In fact, it's so minor that my fellow *Game of Thrones* fanatic friend didn't even realize it happened until I gave my imaginary PowerPoint presentation. So what happens? She takes a bath! AHHHH, right?! But not just any bath! The water is very clearly steaming hot. In fact, as she enters the tub we hear her servant say, "My lady, the water is too hot," but Daenerys still enters without hesitation. And . . . scene.

Are you still with me? I promise this is going somewhere.

Fast-forward a few episodes, and in true *Game of Thrones* fashion, things have escalated quickly. Daenerys's evil brother is killed by molten metal right before her eyes. She watches intently as her brother is burned to death, but her only comment is, "He was no dragon. Fire cannot kill a dragon." And . . . scene.

Stay with me!

For her wedding, Daenerys is gifted with three dragon eggs. These are merely decorative, ancient items, or so it seems. We see Daenerys staring at the eggs while also holding them near a fire. All right, cool. Another moment where Daenerys is in her own world, staring into fire like a lunatic, right? Wrong. The scene ends with her passing the eggs back to her servant . . . except the servant's hands instinctively recoil because the eggs are too hot. She's unable to hold them without getting burned (unlike Daenerys).

So, what's my point?

Daenerys didn't obtain some dragon power one day by luck. She knew she had dragon blood within her all along, but she never told anyone until she could capitalize on that power. While she was being forced into marriage, beaten, and disrespected, she held on to the knowledge that she was the mighty Mother of Dragons. Daenerys kept her strengths and powers a secret from everyone, including her brother and husband, until it was the perfect moment for her to make her move. Had she disclosed her powers from the beginning, her brother might have tried killing her, people might have tried kidnapping her, and she probably wouldn't have been gifted with dragon eggs (that'd be like giving Thor a hammer and expecting him not to use it). Daenerys knew her own power and kept it a secret so that she could deploy that power as effectively as possible. And she uses this strategy repeatedly to get what she wants.

Long story short, if you're selectively secretive, you might become a queen, have dragons, and get to sleep with a very sexy man named Khal Drogo who rides a horse.

Now, I know what you're thinking. Your life isn't *Game of Thrones* and your skill set might not include being the Mother of Dragons (though being really good at Pokémon Go is still pretty cool). Trust me, I get it. At least once a week I get pissed that I don't have dragons. Nor am I suggesting that tolerating abuse is necessary to succeed. What I'm saying is you must think of yourself as a powerful fort. That's how you should view your mind, body, and spirit. You should know all the entrances and secret passageways of your fort, aka your strengths, weaknesses, fears, etc. Feel free to welcome people into your fort for banquets or balls or whatever other fancy party you might have. But the more you tell people about your fort, the more information you reveal about the secret passageways, the weaker your fort becomes and the easier it is for people to attack you. The lesson being: don't give away all your secrets or reveal all your vulnerabilities. Don't trick yourself into believing that you are obligated to share everything with everyone. It's up to you to decide what to reveal and when.

Wow. I guess you were right, Mom. About this, and about me not putting music on your iPod.

I'll do it later. Promise.

"

DON'T
GIVE AWAY
ALL YOUR SECRETS
OR REVEAL ALL
YOUR VULNERABILITIES . . .
IT'S UP TO YOU
TO DECIDE
WHAT TO REVEAL
AND WHEN.

"

CHAPTER 4

GET
UNCOMFORTABLE

SOMEONE SMART ONCE SAID,

"Everything you want is just outside your comfort zone." To be honest, I don't know who said it, so let's just pretend I am that smart person. I said it. Yay me!

(It was actually said by Robert G. Allen, bestselling author, but whatever!)

Being uncomfortable is usually considered a bad thing. When you think of the word "discomfort," you might think of, say, a crowded elevator full of sweaty people, or you might picture a creepy guy who keeps smirking at you from across the room. Or maybe you're watching TV with your parents and Nicki Minaj's music video for "Anaconda" starts playing. Uncomfortable! (Also, why is there a gym in the jungle?)

However, putting yourself in uncomfortable situations is **CRUCIAL** to developing new skills and gaining valuable experience. I know Drake told you he went from "0 to 100 real quick," but I promise you he went from 0 to 1 to 2 to 2.2 to 3. It was only after he put himself in a lot of uncomfortable situations that he finally hit 100. In fact, early in his career, Drake got booed off the stage in his hometown. (Sounds pretty uncomfortable. Also, who boos Drake?!)

I can confidently say that I'm skilled at making YouTube videos, and that's only because I went through the horrifying experience of making my first ten videos. I had to go through the awkward process of figuring out what works and what doesn't. Although it was terrifying, if I hadn't made those first ten videos, I would never have been able to make the 500 videos that are online today and that now have over 1 billion views combined. It's easy to look back and see how far I've come, but it's harder to remember that I need to keep pushing myself. If I know that stepping outside my comfort zone helped me become a YouTube success, then why am I so scared to do it again when auditioning for film roles?

Well, I answered my own question: because it's scary! And sitting in a tense room reciting lines to a complete stranger isn't exactly a comfortable situation.

It's times like these when you need to Bawse up. You have to seek out situations that make you uncomfortable and then throw yourself into them. That doesn't mean risking your life by walking on the edge of a building—you don't need to do everything that scares you or makes you uncomfortable. Instead, push yourself to do things that will help you reach your goal. And if your goal is to walk on the edge of a building, then dude, that's rad as eff. (Also, you're crazy and I want to send your mother an Edible Arrangements basket in sympathy.)

One of my goals is to act in movies. I haven't been to acting school and I don't have much experience on large film sets. So you can imagine my fear when my manager called to tell me I'd been asked to audition for a major role in a high-budget movie. I'd be lying if I said a little pee didn't escape my body.

> **66 YOU HAVE TO SEEK OUT SITUATIONS THAT MAKE YOU UNCOMFORTABLE AND THEN THROW YOURSELF INTO THEM.**

My initial instinct was to say "hell no" because I was terrified and, let's be real, there was zero chance I would land that role. They would definitely want a more experienced and qualified actress to be part of such a huge franchise. I can't say exactly which movie it was (shout-outs to my lawyer), so let's just assume it's a movie about battles that takes place in outer space. Yes, that one. Luckily for me, my schedule conflicted with the audition and I found an excuse not to go. What a lovely, comfortable situation.

Two weeks later my manager phoned me again to say the casting director wanted to book another audition time with me. Now, I'm not a big believer in fate, but when something comes your way twice, you can't help but think Beyoncé, Kelly, and Michelle are in the air because "baby, that's destiny." I mustered up my courage and told them "sure," sealing the deal on my uncomfortable demise.

The morning of the audition I sat down and had a talk with myself. I reminded myself that the first ten times I do anything, I'm horrible at it. BUT those first ten times are crucial in order for me to be successful the eleventh time (or a little better at it). It's not about getting the role; it's about doing the audition. And as long as I leave the audition without having sponta- neously combusted, I will have succeeded.

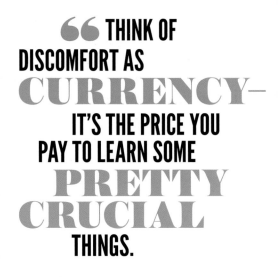

THINK OF DISCOMFORT AS CURRENCY— IT'S THE PRICE YOU PAY TO LEARN SOME PRETTY CRUCIAL THINGS.

I walked into the build- ing and instantly wanted to pass out. It was filled with gorgeous girls who didn't seem to be nervous whatso- ever. I smiled at one and she gave me the cold shoulder. Cue pee escaping body, round two!

I checked in, sat down, and took deep breaths. I didn't get to see any of the script in advance, so I had to learn the entire thing at the audition. Also, minor detail, but I know nothing about this outer space franchise, so reading a script about galaxies with weird names only added to my stress. Is this the name of a main character or did someone sneeze? SEND HELP!

After I'd spent an hour memorizing difficult paragraphs, they called my name and I went into the torture chamb—I mean, audition room. I introduced myself and then the audition quickly began. I started reciting lines, only to mess up a few sentences in. Keep calm, Lilly! Damn, this was really hard, and my brain was racing. But I tried again. Within the space of a few minutes I did the scene twice, and the second time around I didn't forget any of my lines. More importantly, I was still alive!

Afterward the casting agent and I had a great conversation and she told me she was really impressed with my performance. Was she lying? I DON'T CARE. The point is I did it! I DIDN'T SPONTANEOUSLY COM- BUST AS IF HARRY POTTER WERE IN THE CORNER ALL LIKE "REDUCTO." I walked out of that audition and felt amazing. Needless to say, I didn't get the part. I mean, if I was part of a major movie franchise, would I be sitting here in this crappy rented apartment eating two-day-old pizza? No. The answer is no. (Actually . . . maybe.)

Wait. OMG! I get it, Nicki Minaj! There's a gym in the jungle because it's called a jungle gym. Holy crap, I'm a genius.

Back to my point. The next time I have a difficult audition I'm going to feel a tad better about it because of this experience. It'll keep getting a little easier and a little less terrifying each time. To succeed at something, you have to step out of your comfort zone, inch by inch. Think of discomfort as currency—it's the price you pay to learn some pretty crucial things. Besides, the goal isn't always the trophy. The goal can also be the stepping-stones—the bronze and silver medals that bring you closer to the gold.

Remember, on the path to success, fear and discomfort are only speed bumps. Don't make them dead ends.

May the gravity be with you. Wait, that's how it goes, right?

Get Uncomfortable

What are three things you know you need to do in order to succeed, but find absolutely terrifying?

1. _____

_____

2. _____

_____

3. _____

_____

CHAPTER 5

HAVE FEWER EMOTIONS

EMOTIONS ARE GREAT

if you're at a wedding, a funeral, or your kid's graduation or while watching *The Lion King*. It's a wonderful blessing to be in situations that evoke real emotion. Your baby girl is walking onstage looking like an adult, being handed her diploma, and you shed a tear. She's all grown up now. Also, her tuition fees left you broke and now your TV is an iPod with a magnifying glass in front of it. It's all so overwhelming and bittersweet. You should cry your heart out. But when you're in a situation in which work needs to get done, put those emotions away. Emotions can cloud your judgment and reduce productivity. That's not my opinion; it's a fact. A fact that I made up just now, but it's probably 100 percent scientifically accurate.

I'm not suggesting you be a heartless robot, but I *am* encouraging you to have selective emotions when tasks need to get done, especially in a group setting. Maybe there are ten valid reasons to be upset with your life right now, but in the middle of a shoot, with a crew of ten people who all have a job to get done, getting angry or offended will not help. It's extremely difficult to do, but a Bawse understands the importance of having tunnel vision. Sometimes you have to block out distracting emotions in order to get things done, especially if other team members are relying on you.

I get a little (aka very) crazy when I'm in creation mode. I want to make magic, and when I'm calling the shots I practice a tunnel vision so intense that my peripherals couldn't even sense a bird flying toward my head. It's a blessing and a curse. Beaks are sharp. I have more ear piercings than I'd like.

When I was on the set of my music video "#LEH," my friend and co-producer Humble and I were on the same page when it came to craziness. Like me, he's very goal-oriented and believes that limiting your range of emotions will go a long way when you're trying to complete a task. That's why we work so well together. We both act like the Tin Man from *The Wizard of Oz* when we're on set—no heart, all determination. The only difference is that we couldn't care less about Dorothy unless she's involved with our project. However, we understand that not everyone is like that.

Before we started shooting we had a meeting with the entire cast and crew in hopes of setting a certain tone on set. We made it very clear that we had a deadline and time was NOT on our side. We were trying to shoot an entire music video featuring a lot of moving parts—cars, extras, props, and several costume changes—in just a few hours. As a result, communication on set was going to be very blunt and to the point because we didn't have time for pleasantries. We also made it clear that everything that happened while shooting, from a director yelling to a scene needing to be redone, would be for the benefit of the project. The completion of the project would be our only priority for the next few hours and no one had any other side agendas. If you got yelled at, it was because things needed to get done faster, for the good of the project, not because someone wanted to upset Kim. No one has "upset Kim" on their to-do list. So, Kim, don't trip.

The result was a very efficient shoot. Yes, people got yelled at, including me (by Humble, and vice versa), but no one's feelings were hurt. We were lucky to have a team of people who were able to put their emotions to the side for the day, but that's not always the case.

While I was on tour last year, I faced some very stressful situations. Sometimes, just moments before a show, a costume would go missing, a dancer wasn't ready, or, better yet, my earpiece would stop working. Before one show, one of my crew members got frustrated and started crying because she couldn't access a dressing room. When anyone would try to help she would brush them off and say she was "fine," which she was clearly not. In a situation where fourteen other people are relying on you to do your part and get work done, emotions are the last thing you want to display. Not only does it create a negative energy, but it also affects your work.

Now, you might be thinking that I sound like a total jerk, and that's fair. Humans have emotions and they cannot always control them. The thing is, I am not suggesting that you become mechanical and turn off your heart. I am suggesting that you train your brain to focus less on feelings and more on productivity when

66 WHEN YOU NEED TO GET YOUR HUSTLE ON, BE DRIVEN BY GOALS, NOT EMOTIONS.

things need to get done. When you need to get your hustle on, be driven by goals, not emotions. When you're working with a group and feel any type of negative emotion, ask yourself, "Does this emotion help get the task done?" If not, then put it away. Sometimes we get angry or annoyed at people we're working with, and so we retaliate. Ask yourself again, does retaliation help get the task done? It's a hard pill to swallow, but in the battle between pride versus productivity, sometimes you need to let your pride lose. It's not about rights and wrongs when you have two hours left to capture four more hours of footage; it's about getting it done.

MAKE EVERY STRUGGLE COUNT AND REMEMBER THAT EXPERIENCE WILL ALWAYS BE A SILVER LINING.

A perfect example of someone who has a handle on their emotions when it counts is my day-to-day manager, Kyle. He's a recent member of my team and hopefully, by the time you're reading this, he's still kicking it with me and hasn't left me to become president of the world (which is very possible). Don't get it twisted—Kyle is very emotional. In fact, on our trip to Kenya, he was the first to cry during our nightly reflections. Twice. But when it comes to work, Kyle is great at putting his emotions and pride away and getting the job done. When there is some miscommunication within my team that results in a mistake, Kyle will apologize even if it's not his fault. There have been many times when an issue has had nothing to do with Kyle, but he recognized the stress it brought to me and apologized anyway while he helped figure out a solution. He recognizes that reducing my stress allows me to be my best creative self, which is beneficial to everyone on the team. Productivity over pride. Elevation over ego.

If you're in a situation where you've completed a task successfully and still feel uncomfortable with the way someone treated or talked to you, then by all means communicate it to them. No one is asking you to be a doormat. You should be comfortable telling people how you'd like to be treated. Just don't have this conversation in the middle of a chaotic work situation. Can you imagine an entire crew running around, paperwork flying everywhere, seven people yelling how much time we have left, and, in the middle of all that, having someone approach you and say, "I'd like to talk to you about how I feel right now"? This is not *Full House*. Do not cue the sentimental music. There's a time and a place.

From a professional standpoint, we've established it's best not to let your inner emojis affect your productivity, but what about from a personal standpoint? In this case, we can be a little more lenient because no one is relying on you to get work done, except you (and maybe your parents, if you live at home). Do I believe you should have fewer emotions when dealing with personal struggles? Well, yes . . . and no. No, because emotions need to be felt and it's not healthy to bottle up pain. I believe in crying your eyes out instead of having pent-up anger. But, I'd also argue that, yes, having TOO many emotions can blind us to the life lessons we could be learning when things fall apart.

Basically, I believe in getting hurt *efficiently*.

This means that I thoroughly believe in crying, yelling, pulling my hair out, and experiencing heartache, BUT once I'm done I dissect the pain and learn lessons from it. Heartache is never going to go away and every person will continue to experience it. Not learning anything from pain because you are too overwhelmed with emotion is inefficient, especially since you'll continue to encounter pain in life. When you get hurt, use that hurt as body armor for future battles. That doesn't mean close yourself off and turn into an ice queen (or king); it simply means you should reason with yourself and try to remember that getting hurt today makes you more resilient tomorrow. Pain is good. Heartache is good. These things provide you with knowledge that will help you grow and deal with future struggles. To waste a painful moment and let emotion overwhelm you so much that you gain absolutely no insight is to get hurt inefficiently. Make every struggle count and remember that experience will *always* be a silver lining.

There are so many reasons to get emotional in life. Phoebe and Joey didn't end up together in the series finale of *Friends*. During his speech at the MTV Video Music Awards, Drake admitted to being in love with Rihanna since he was twenty-two. He was twenty-nine when he said those words. That's seven years in the friend zone. The original yellow Power Ranger no longer walks this earth. Three iPhone releases from now, Apple will yet again change the shape of the charging port and we'll all cave and buy new accessories. If you want to cry over every mildly upsetting thing to ever occur in your spare time, feel free (although that sounds exhausting). When it comes to getting work done and having the opportunity to learn lessons, don't let your emotions rob you.

CHAPTER 6

DON'T OVERTHINK

THINKING IS GREAT.

I love thinking. I bet teddy bears are so pissed that they can't think like us. Except Ted, obviously. Speaking of which, *Ted* is a great example of not overthinking since it's a movie about a talking bear who gets married to a human woman. #LoveWins. Unfortunately, though, we don't always follow our gut. Sometimes when we're passionate about something or in some kind of bind, we tend to think a lot about the "what, where, when, how, and why" of the situation, to the point that it becomes unproductive. It happens to the best of us. Overthinking is a natural enemy of efficiency because it prevents us from getting things done. A Bawse should know when to take the time to think something through and when to simply make a quick decision.

Going in circles will never get you anywhere (unless you're the Earth, in which case you're alllriighhhttt). For example, your boyfriend tells you he wants to talk. Before you call him, you spend forty-five minutes thinking about how the conversation will play out. *What if he cheated on me? What if I accidentally cheated on him and I didn't realize it? Maybe I was drunk? Maybe he has pictures? Maybe I'm on TMZ! Or what if he has cancer? OMG! He's actually a robot. I knew it. I'm dating the robot from* Big Hero 6! None of these thoughts are helpful. What you need to do is simply pick up the phone and call your boyfriend. And when you do, you may feel silly and realize how much time you wasted worrying when he asks, "Can you drive tonight?"

When it comes to creating my weekly YouTube content, I try my best not to overthink it. I could never make two videos a week if I sat at my desk and thought about every single frame, shot, and sentence over and over again. My weekly videos would turn into yearly videos. Therefore, when I partner up with companies to shoot branded content, it's always a little bit of a struggle on my part. For legal reasons, I understand why companies have to focus on minor details and chew them over. People love to sue, especially in America! I also understand that companies have big production budgets, so they feel obligated to spend money on all the small details that I don't think are all that important when it comes to online content. We're from different worlds.

I remember one particular video shoot that followed a very basic story line. I was supposed to do an intro, surprise someone, and have a conversation with them. Easy peasy, lemon squeezy. The next few hours were spent shooting this very simple video even though the shoot could have easily gotten done in thirty minutes. Why did it take so long? The set designer was constantly adjusting a plant or vase that would end up completely blurred out in the background of the shot. The videographer wanted three different shots of a basic motion. Now, all of this is fine. I get it—you have cool toys you want to play with. But simply having the ability and equipment to do something doesn't justify that it should be done. And all of this overthinking was causing the story line to suffer. There were times when I was the only person in the room who had the ability to say, "Ummm, hey, that shot ruins the entire surprise." The response would be, "OH YEAH! . . . that."

The story should be the priority, first and foremost. Can the audience follow what's happening? Are we making it clear? Because if we aren't, then it doesn't matter if this Steadicam shot with strobe lights and a well-positioned plant in the background look great. It's important to recognize when time is being wasted and to take a step back. Taking a step back is so important. In fact, we should make it a viral dance video online. TAKE A STEP BACK, NOW TAKE A STEP BACK. AYYYEEE! I can already see it hitting a billion views.

Oh wait, I guess that's similar to "Lean Back" by Fat Joe. Fine. Whatever. Take away my joy, Joe.

Humans have a tendency to overcomplicate simple things because we overthink them. But if you take a step back and remember your priorities, it becomes easier to make a decision. When you're in these situations, I encourage you to ask yourself basic questions while keeping your priorities in mind. If you care about money, ask yourself, "Does this job pay well?" If you care about mental health, ask yourself, "Does this job make me happy?" Ask questions that align with your priorities and ignore all the other noise. If your priority is an amazing product, it doesn't matter if fourteen people worked hard on it or if you spent a ton of time on it. The question you should ask is, "Is this an amazing product?," then base your next actions on that answer. Sometimes we overthink something to avoid

"

HUMANS HAVE A TENDENCY
TO OVERCOMPLICATE **SIMPLE THINGS BECAUSE WE** OVERTHINK **THEM.
BUT IF YOU** TAKE A STEP BACK **AND REMEMBER YOUR** PRIORITIES, **IT BECOMES EASIER TO MAKE A** DECISION.

"

the fact that there is no feel-good decision to make. The first time I had a major problem with one of my employees, I drove myself crazy over-thinking the issue. *Why do they keep making this mistake? What can I do differently? How can I penalize them? How can I train them better?* I went to bed every night thinking, *There's just no solution to this problem.* But, in reality, the solution was to fire them. I just didn't like that solution, and therefore I refused to consider it. But overthinking things didn't help them or me. Sometimes the right thing is also the hard thing.

The next time you find yourself going around in circles, ask yourself, are you a Ferris wheel? What about a merry-go-round? Can you please confirm that you are not a merry-go-round? I'm assuming you are not (if so, jealous! Ponies are dope). In that case, stop going around in circles and instead take advantage of your valuable time and make some tough deci-sions. Step out of the complicated maze you've created and take a one-way street to Clarityville. Things can be simple when you take a step back.

TAKE A STEP BACK. NOW TAKE A STEP BACK.

Eff it. Fat Joe, I am coming for you.

CHAPTER 7

CALL
YOURSELF
OUT

MAKING MISTAKES IS COOL.

There seems to be this misconception that making mistakes makes you weak, or stupid, or somehow less of a person, but the truth is, making mistakes brings you one step closer to success. No one has the answer key to life and so when we want to accomplish anything, whether it's learning a new braid or becoming the CEO of a marketing company, we must make mistakes along the way. It's the only way we can learn what works and what doesn't. The person who invented the first phone didn't create an iPhone 7, and I'm sure the first person to invent the parachute had a few bruises. If you're making mistakes, you're making the necessary moves to figuring it all out. If you think there are ten possible ways to do something and you just made a mistake, congratulations. You've just discovered that #4 doesn't work. That's progress! If you're not making mistakes, you're not taking any steps toward accomplishing a goal. Mistakes. Are. Cool.

Mistakes don't exist just to make us feel bad about ourselves; they are opportunities that we should not ignore or shy away from. People pay thousands of dollars in tuition to learn lessons at college, while all the time mistakes are lingering around for free, ready to school us. The goal is to recognize our mistakes, learn from them, and try to prevent them in the future. To do this, I've come up with four important steps.

1 TAKE OWNERSHIP

Taking ownership of a mistake is like attending a class—it's the only way you'll learn something from it. If you cannot admit to a mistake, you're skipping school and wasting your tuition. Owning up is difficult for a lot of people because it requires disarming defense mechanisms such as pride, fear, and ego, just to name a few. As a result, people resort to insane behaviors to address mistakes without taking the hit. For example, if you were supposed to submit a project by 4:00 P.M., here are a few common ways to NOT take ownership:

BLAME GAME:

"I didn't hand in the project because Carl from human resources didn't remind me. He said he would."

DEFLECT:

"Well, Samantha didn't hand in her project either."

DENY:

"I didn't know there was a project due today."

IGNORE:

(At 7:00 P.M.) "Here's my project. Bye."

Not only is this behavior frustrating for people who work with you, it robs you of the power to come up with a solution. If you admit to making a mistake, you can work on fixing it, but if you deny the entire thing, who's going to solve the issue? A Bawse does not use defense mechanisms to get out of cleaning up a mess they made. Nor do they take half ownership for things. Here's an example of half ownership:

HALF OWNERSHIP:

"Hey, I'm sorry my project is late. Carl was supposed to remind me, but he didn't. But even still, I'm really sorry."

BAWSE OWNERSHIP:

"I know the project was due at 4:00 P.M. and it is now 7:00 P.M. For that I am sorry and no excuse is valid."

② CALL YOURSELF OUT

If you didn't hand in the project on time, ask yourself why, before someone else does. You should know yourself best, so why wait until someone else calls you out to scramble to find the answer? Before you answer to your boss, answer to your inner Bawse. You should want to identify the cause of your mistake so that you can understand how to prevent it, not because your supervisor is going to need an explanation. And when you give yourself a reason for why you made a mistake, be real and honest. I say this because sometimes we use the best defense mechanisms against ourselves. For example, you might tell yourself you didn't do the project because you didn't have enough time. That might be true. But what did you do instead? Did you go to a party? Did you hang out with a boyfriend? Did you binge-watch *Orange Is the New Black?* If you're nodding your head, then that's the real reason you didn't hand in your project. You didn't prioritize your work. When you make mistakes, call yourself out honestly. Honesty is the new black.

66 MISTAKES DON'T **EXIST** JUST TO MAKE US **FEEL BAD** ABOUT OURSELVES; THEY **ARE** OPPORTUNITIES THAT WE SHOULD NOT **IGNORE** OR **SHY** AWAY FROM.

3 FIND SOLUTIONS

Mistakes are valuable only if you discover how to prevent them from happening again. If your next three projects are all late, then you didn't really learn much from your mistake, did you? Once you honestly identify the cause of your mistake, come up with a solution. If the reason is that you didn't have enough time, then make a schedule that gives you enough time. Create a reward system that allows you to go to a party only if you finish x amount of work. You cannot keep doing the same thing and expect different results. That's the definition of insanity. You need to find solutions, and not just fairy-tale solutions like "try harder" but real solutions like "cancel my monthly subscription." Snap! Ish just got real!

4 COMMUNICATE

Once you learn how to take ownership, call yourself out honestly, and find solutions, you can learn to apologize efficiently, in a meaningful way. No mistake is too big or too small to apologize for, and no ego should be too big to make that apology. The biggest mistake you can make is thinking an apology doesn't matter. An apology indicates that you care and, to be blunt, that you're a responsible adult—not a six-year-old child. So whether you did something small, like forget to respond to an email, or something much larger, like hurt a friend, take the time to deliver an honest apology and explain how you'll prevent your mistake from happening again in the future.

WACK APOLOGY:

I'm sorry. Next time I won't ask Carl to remind me about the project. When he forgets it's frustrating for everyone.

Nah, you can do better than that. Stop being wacksauce.

BAWSE APOLOGY:

"I'm sorry my project is late. I take complete ownership for the delay. I've already come up with ways to ensure I get things done on time in the future. You can expect better."

All right, Carl. You're off the hook.

Whether receiving an award or admitting to a mistake, a Bawse will stand up tall because they understand that both contribute toward growth and progress. When you have the guts to make mistakes, great things happen. And when you have the integrity to take ownership of those mistakes, the people around you will take notice. So eff up, empower your inner referee, call yourself out, and move one step closer to success.

CHAPTER 8

SEND THE GPS DEEP

SOMETIMES I'M MIDWAY

through my day and I discover I have a stain on my shirt. And by "sometimes" I mean daily, because I'm an animal. So what do I do? I cover it with a jacket or decorative pin. Problem solved. Similarly, when I have a pimple (also almost daily), I cover it with concealer. When I spill my drink on the carpet and the stain won't go away, I buy a new plant and conveniently place it on top. It works out great until I spill my drink four more times and my living room looks like something out of *Jumanji*.

For most slip-ups in life, it's easy to find solutions that simply cover up the problem. But when it comes to your professional, personal, and behavioral problems, a cover-up won't cut it. You need to go beyond blanket solutions and get to the root of the problem. You should know yourself so well that it would be easy to draw an IKEA instruction manual for yourself (yes, I said "IKEA instruction manual" and "easy" in the same sentence. There's a first time for everything). Part of conquering your mind (see the chapter Conquer Your Thoughts) and knowing yourself is sending the GPS deep and addressing your inner issues.

When it comes to understanding our behavior and why we do the things we do, I believe each of us has a minimum of three layers. Surprise, you're a tiramisu! The top layer consists of how we explain ourselves and our actions to other people. This is the easiest layer of the tiramisu to digest because it's light and fluffy and makes the dessert look pretty. The middle layer consists of how we explain our actions to ourselves. This layer is a bit heavier and deeper, and oftentimes you can't see it from the outside because it's just below the whipped cream. Finally, we reach the bottom layer, which consists of the deeply rooted reasons we actually behave the way we do. This layer is the hardest to find because it's buried deep within your tiramisu and so you have to push aside all the other layers to discover it. It doesn't always taste the best and it's definitely not the prettiest, but it's the foundation of the entire dessert.

Now that I've made you hungry and you want to take a bite of your own arm, let me show you what I mean with an example from my own life.

BEHAVIOR:

I tell everyone that I don't want to be in a relationship right now.

LAYER 1: WHAT I TELL OTHER PEOPLE

I'm too busy hustling and sipping that #Lemonade that Beyoncé served. I don't need a man. *snaps fingers*

LAYER 2: WHAT I TELL MYSELF

I love my career way too much and don't have time to waste on a relationship. That type of commitment would hold me back from achieving my dreams. I don't want to be tied down.

LAYER 3: THE ACTUAL REASON

I don't know how to have a successful relationship while pursuing my dreams, and so when I sense a potential relationship, I run away. I'm scared a relationship will negatively impact me, regardless of who it's with.

Discovering layer three has helped me take the first step toward having healthier relationships. After digging deeper and analyzing my childhood, I discovered that my desire to be single isn't because I love Beyoncé and enjoy independence. I mean, sure, those are factors, but they aren't the real reasons. The real reason is that I'm scared of relationships.

Remember when I said that I believe we all have a MINIMUM of three layers? That's because oftentimes there is a deeper, hidden fourth layer that can only be discovered over time. As we grow older, experience new things, and are introduced to new ideas, layers start to melt away and a deeper understanding of ourselves is revealed.

LAYER 4: DOWN TO THE INGREDIENTS OF THE TIRAMISU

I was never exposed to healthy relationships growing up and so I don't believe they actually exist. I think relationships bring out the worst in people, no matter what.

I rarely give my relationships a fighting chance, and the discovery of layer four really helped me understand why. Sending the GPS deep allowed me to recognize my own irrational thought processes and take active steps toward working on them. It's also important to note that it's completely normal to have irrational, deep-rooted thoughts. You shouldn't feel bad or embarrassed about the lessons you were exposed to growing up. We're all a little crazy and messed up in our own special way *licks glue*.

Here is another example from my personal life:

BEHAVIOR:

I surround myself with colors and positive quotes.

LAYER 1: WHAT I TELL OTHER PEOPLE

I'm a unicorn that loves to be happy!

LAYER 2: WHAT I TELL MYSELF

I love myself and want to be happy. I want to surround myself with things that make me feel good so I can be my best self.

LAYER 3: THE REAL REASON

I know what it feels like to be sad and I'm terrified to feel that way again. I need to take every measure to ensure that I'm in a good place as often as possible.

Addressing your inner issues not only is a liberating experience but also allows you to begin creating meaningful solutions. In the above example, it was only after I discovered layer three that I was able to address the issue honestly. If I have a deep-rooted FEAR of sadness and I feel like I NEED to always be happy, the surface solution is to surround myself with fluffy quotes. But the real solution is to become comfortable with all my emotions, whether they are positive or negative. This realization helped me learn how to love myself and my life even when I'm sad. It taught me that it's okay to be sad and that one bad day doesn't equal full-fledged depression. Over time, I've learned to associate sadness with emotional growth and awareness instead of terror. This wouldn't have been possible if I kept eating the whipped cream off the tiramisu and throwing the rest away. Eat all your dessert, kids!

A lot of times we're scared to address our inner issues because we don't think we'll find a way to fix them. Sometimes solutions can be found with just a little time, effort, and creativity. But at other times our fear is absolutely valid because there isn't a solution. I'm not naive enough to think that every deep-rooted issue is solvable, but perhaps the only solution is to simply be self-aware. If there's a leaky faucet in your soul that you've tried over and over again to fix but you simply cannot, buy a bucket, warn people about the leak, and be prepared to get a little wet. After all, none of us are perfect.

For example, I know loyalty is a huge issue for me. I've done the tiramisu analysis and there are several reasons why I have a hard time forgiving dishonesty. I've made many efforts to fix this issue, and although I've progressed a little, I still struggle with it. As a result, whenever I get into a relationship, I openly tell the other person that I simply CANNOT forgive someone who is not loyal. It's not that I don't WANT TO; I simply don't know how to. That way, if disloyalty becomes an issue, no one is surprised by how I'll react. At least when my issues are out in the open, they can be discussed and taken into account. That's my bucket for a leaky faucet.

Understanding yourself and why you are the way you are requires complete honesty. So pull out your magnifying glass and take a look at the molecules that make up your unique existence. You're like Sherlock Holmes and this is your most important investigation.

Now, if you'll excuse me, I spilled another drink on my carpet and need to buy a cactus.

Try It

Why do you work hard? Or why do you not work hard? Dig deep and discover your layers.

Layer 1: _____

_____

Layer 2: _____

_____

Layer 3: _____

_____

Possible Layer 4: _____

_____

CHAPTER 9

EXERCISE SELF-CONTROL

SELF-CONTROL

is one of the most important muscles a Bawse can have. Just like any other muscle in your body, self-control needs to be worked if it's going to get stronger. Unfortunately, there are probably so many other things you would rather do than work your self-cont—Hold on, what's this notification? OMG, stop it. Sorry, one sec. My friend just posted an engagement picture on Facebook and I'm experiencing all the bittersweet feels. When did this even happen?! The last time I hung out with her, her ringtone was "Single Ladies." Oh look, there's an albu—Wait, "10 Things Successful People Do Every Day." Let me check out this BuzzFeed article real quick. It says I won't believe number four! What's number four? SHOW ME NUMBER FOUR.

three hours later

As I was saying, it's important to exercise self-control if you want to complete tasks. But let's be real—that's easier said than done. How do you obtain self-control? And how do you continue to work it and make it stronger? After all, there's a lot of temptation out there to distract you from doing your work, and it's easier to give in to temptation than to fight it. Well, you have to create a workout plan that's right for you.

Here are three exercises to help build your self-control.

1 SET GOALS FOR YOURSELF

If you have to get something done, there are several ways you can set goals for yourself. One way is to create a schedule and try completing a task by a certain time. For example, when writing this book, each time I'd start writing, I'd give myself x amount of time to finish a chapter. Then I'd try my best to not only meet but beat that goal. If I finished five minutes before my goal, I would allow myself to spend those five minutes doing whatever I wanted to do. Five minutes of dancing to old-school Bollywood music in my sports bra before starting the next chapter? Don't mind if

I do! (Also, sorry neighbors!) I would only be allowed to do this leisure activity if I beat my goal. The more time I beat it by, the more time I had for dancing.

Another way to set a goal is to tell yourself you'll finish x amount of tasks before you're done working for the day. For example, when I'm sorting through the Superwoman inbox (it's like quicksand in there), I'll tell myself that I can take a break after sorting through 200 emails.

Setting goals requires you to work efficiently. Telling yourself that you have to finish something by a certain time or after a certain number of tasks lights a fire under your hustle.

2 REWARD YOURSELF

Once you set a goal, it's important to reward yourself when you hit it. A reward can be a break in between tasks (like eating a yummy snack or watching a funny iiSuperwomanii video . . . heyyy), or you can give yourself a bigger reward for completing all your work at the end of the day. Make sure your rewards are well-earned and reasonable. You don't want to finish two emails and then allow yourself to take a four-hour nap. That doesn't make any sense. For example, after writing three chapters today, I'm allowed to watch an hour of Netflix, and therefore I shall type at the speed of light.

The reward system will work as motivation only as long as you don't cheat. If I write only two chapters today, I can't allow myself to watch an hour of Netflix. I guess it takes some self-control to implement self-control. One way of getting around this issue is by putting your reward in the hands of someone else. For example, I could tell my friend to change my Netflix password and only give it to me when I present them with three chapters. This might result in a heated argument when I'm sleepy after finishing two chapters, but it keeps me honest!

Other ideas include:

- Getting your friend to change your social media passwords until you're done studying

- Letting a friend confiscate your phone until you're done working

- Getting someone to change your Wi-Fi password until you're done working out (THE HORROR!)

③ CHALLENGE YOURSELF

When you want to strengthen a muscle, you gradually increase your reps or the weight of the dumbbell. You can apply the same principle when exercising self-control. For example, I don't swear. I don't think anything is wrong with swearing—in fact, I thoroughly enjoy it when other people do it—but I just prefer not to. Of course I have the temptation to swear; I mean, I watch *Game of Thrones*. Red wedding, hello! I wanted to swear for sixty minutes straight after that. But not swearing is something I choose to control, and to be honest, making that choice has helped me exercise self-control in other areas of my life. Not swearing has made me better at not gossiping, not spilling secrets, and not saying something impulsively during an interview.

You don't have to suddenly decide to change something in your life to exercise self-control, but you can set challenges for yourself. Think of a habit you'd like to break and give yourself mini training sessions.

Here are some ideas:

- If you're potty-mouthed, don't swear for twenty-four hours. If you fail, reset your time.

- If you are a major carnivore, become a vegetarian for two days. If you fail, reset your time.

- If you nibble on your fingers, don't bite your nails for a day. If you fail, reset your time.

I'm not trying to imply that swearing is wrong and people who eat meat are bad. That's not what this is about. This is about challenging yourself to control something that has become a habit. The more you do this, the better you'll be at exhibiting self-control in other areas of your life, like procrastinating and getting lost on BuzzFeed. I promise you, number four isn't ever that exciting!

When you find ways to work your self-control muscle, you'll develop stamina. When I moved to L.A., there was a period of two months when I didn't have an assistant. As a result, my workload doubled and I had to work twice as hard to keep my business from falling apart. One of the most difficult tasks was editing my daily vlogs, something my assistant would usually do. After I'd been working for hours on a scripted video, the idea of spending twenty minutes to edit a vlog seemed torturous. But every night I would crawl into bed, open my laptop, and edit the vlog. Tears of exhaustion would stream down my cheeks. But pushing myself for those last twenty minutes not only made the reward of sleep so incredibly sweet but also helped me hustle that much harder throughout the day. Suddenly I could write a script for twenty more minutes before calling it quits. I could write ten more emails than usual before turning off my computer. Whereas before I would ignore the sink full of dishes before going to sleep, now I was suddenly rolling up my sleeves and getting the job done. I was flexing my self-control muscle like THE BEACH IS THAT WAY!

Here's a little food for thought: If you're constantly struggling to exercise self-control when it comes to finishing your work, maybe it's time to question your work. A lot of people ask me how I'm able to work twelve hours straight on a task, and this question always confuses me. I don't feel like I'm always pushing myself, and that's because I enjoy what I do. When you like what you do, you're motivated to keep doing it. In other words, a very basic way of having self-control is to do something you like.

Behind every successful person is a relentless work ethic, the ability to block out distractions, and a well-defined six-pack of self-control. Find creative ways to work your self-control and keep making it stronger. Unlike your abs, this muscle needs to be fit even during the winter, so get to work.

Now, if you'll excuse me, I have some sweet, sweet Netflix to watch.

Let's Work

Make a list of self-control challenges that work for you. Start with a twenty-four-hour challenge and work your way up from there.

1. _____

_____

2. _____

_____

3. _____

_____

CHAPTER 10

DON'T
SURVIVE

TAKE A LOOK AROUND.

Are you in the middle of the ocean? Did your ship just sink? If you're unsure, please check your iCal to determine if you recently boarded the *Titanic*. If yes, please try harder to fit two people on that floating door because I promise you it's possible. At the very least, you could take turns so no one has to die. If your answer is no, you're not on the *Titanic,* then why are you acting as if you need to survive life right now? If you're able to read this book, chances are you have been blessed with the tools necessary within and around you to not just survive life but conquer it.

Earlier in my life I didn't know the difference between surviving and conquering. I didn't think it mattered how I completed a task, as long as I achieved what I needed to achieve. It wasn't until I went on my first tour that I learned what a difference it can make not just to do something to get by but to do something to make a statement. My tour consisted of thirty-one shows in twenty-six cities across the world, and as you can imagine, it was exhausting, both mentally and physically. The first few shows were in India, truly across the planet, in a different time zone with different food and an extremely different climate to adjust to. These were all additional challenges to the already difficult task of putting on a good show. Our tour started with six back-to-back shows in different cities within India, each requiring a plane ride to get to. When you begin a tour under these conditions you can't help but enter survival mode immediately. As a result, for the first eight or so shows of my tour, I acted like a character on *The Walking Dead*. Before going onstage I would say to myself, "Okay, just get through this show, Lilly. You can survive this." I'd walk onstage, the crowd would cheer, I would go through the motions very carefully and play it safe, and then two hours later I'd walk offstage feeling great about surviving another run.

This went on for the first few shows until, before my ninth show, I tried something new. I was feeling myself that day and I could hear the crowd going wild well before the show was scheduled to start. I don't know if it was because of the extra sleep I might have gotten the night before or if I'd eaten some particularly delicious french fries that day, but a voice inside me said, "You know what? Don't just go out there and go through the motions. Go out there and absolutely kill it." I promised myself that I would deliver my jokes better than ever before, nail my choreography with complete confidence, and put on the most charismatic show of my life. I wouldn't simply check this show off my list; I would go out there and change lives. I riled myself up, chugged some water, made a pinky promise to myself, and ran out onto the stage. The energy was explosive as I jumped with excitement during parts of my choreography, something I've never done before. My dancers noticed and their excitement and energy increased tenfold as well. I added another layer of flair and fun to my jokes. I made my faces a little sillier, moved my body a little goofier, and held my pauses a little longer. When I made my motivational speech toward the end of the show, I didn't just recite the lines but truly felt each word I was saying with intense emotion.

Two hours later I finished the show, and as our tradition called for, my dancers received me at the side of the stage with open arms. Even though the show was over, I could sense a new type of excitement from them because they felt the new energy I had brought that evening. The crowd's reaction was bigger than it had been at any of our previous shows, and we all felt it in our veins. Of course, I was twice as exhausted, but I was also twice as proud, and I'd had twice as much fun than ever before. From then on, my pre-show pep talk wasn't about survival—it was about conquering. At each show I would move energetically around the stage, laugh at my own jokes, and connect with people. At the beginning of each show I would think of new ways to do it bigger and better. Sometimes I would add a line to my script or change something up just to give my dancers some shock and excitement onstage.

Learning how to conquer my show took hard work. Taking my show to the next level meant knowing my choreography better than ever before, being absolutely fluent with my stand-up material, and fine-tuning my ability to improv for a specific audience and culture. All that meant more rehearsal, more creativity, and more sacrifices when it came to leisure activities. It meant not celebrating after a show in order to get extra sleep. It meant overcoming nerves and fear to make sure confidence and passion were the only things I felt before I stepped onto that stage.

Having said all that, life can be really tough sometimes. Maybe you're forced to enter survival mode because you have financial problems. Maybe you're limited by your physical or mental health. It's hard to think about conquering life when you're trying to overcome an illness and struggling to pay the bills. Realistically, we all have to go into survival mode sometimes because our life circumstances demand it. And that's okay. But too often I feel we stay in this mindset instead of taking control of our life and enjoying it. There is a switch within all of us that we can flick from SURVIVE to CONQUER. Even though we need to survive sometimes, we shouldn't get too comfortable in our life jackets.

Don't just try to pass your classes; try to ace them. Don't just aim to pay your bills; save enough to travel. I don't want you to write a script just to see a movie get made; I want you to win an Oscar. That's the difference between settling like a survivor and conquering like a Bawse.

So if you're drowning, keep your life jacket on and fight. But once you're able to swim, don't convince yourself you forgot how to. Take your life jacket off, front-crawl your way to the shore, walk off that beach, and set your GPS to the top of a hill, because you **WILL** conquer the climb.

If you're going to do it, do it the best you possibly can.

"

DON'T JUST TRY **TO PASS YOUR CLASSES;** TRY TO ACE THEM. **DON'T JUST AIM TO PAY YOUR BILLS;** SAVE ENOUGH TO TRAVEL. **I DON'T WANT YOU TO** WRITE A SCRIPT JUST TO **SEE A MOVIE GET MADE; I WANT YOU TO** WIN AN OSCAR. **THAT'S THE DIFFERENCE BETWEEN** SETTLING LIKE A SURVIVOR **AND CONQUERING** LIKE A BAWSE.

"

CHAPTER 11

BE IN LOVE

‹------------------------------›

BEING IN LOVE

is exciting. We get that tingly feeling in our toes and we have someone to text goodnight. We want the people we love to be happy and we truly wish the best for them. When they succeed we feel proud of them, and when they struggle we want to help them. We're even willing to buy a completely new shirt that is one shade brighter than the one we currently have, so that we can be weird lover twins in exact matching outfits. Ruby red and cherry red are very different when you're in love, okay?

Romantic comedies, lovey-dovey novels, and the majority of love songs have all gotten us used to the idea that our love is meant for other people. We even have specific days dedicated to loving specific people: anniversaries are for lovers, Mother's Day is for mothers, Father's Day is for fathers, and Valentine's Day is for florists. But love shouldn't just be reserved for other people. First and foremost, you must learn to love yourself. It's only when you love yourself that you can truly love others. When you don't love yourself, you will project your insecurities and internal issues onto others, preventing you from ever genuinely seeing them for who they are. In addition, if you don't love yourself, you're probably not the happiest version of yourself, and thus you're unable to love someone to the best of your ability.

You might be wondering, "Okay, honestly, does loving yourself really relate to being a Bawse?" And my response is, "It relates so much that they're basically first cousins." Loving yourself means you care about yourself. And someone who is well taken care of is more likely to be happy, healthy, and productive. Loving yourself means wanting to make yourself proud. Loving yourself means consoling yourself and encouraging yourself when you face failure, which you inevitably will. And most importantly, loving yourself means that you advocate for yourself, ensuring that you're treated the way a Bawse should be treated.

I didn't always love myself. I had to fall in love with myself, and it was a really awkward first date. There I was, depressed and wanting to end my life, unmotivated, and scared. When you're all alone, not by force but by choice, because you don't feel any desire to be around anyone, the only person you have to rely on is yourself. I don't know what caused me to do it, nor do I know how I convinced myself to, but on one of my worst nights, I started to hug myself. I felt so sorry for myself and for how I was feeling. I could almost see myself as a character in a movie, and my natural reaction was to wrap my arms around myself. After all, that's what you do when you see someone who's sad, right? I hugged myself to sleep and survived the night.

Over the next few weeks, I kept taking myself out on dates, and I began to grow to like myself. I wasn't a sad, pathetic loser after all. I realized there might actually be some depth and spark within me. I began talking to myself a lot more often and I thought about myself spontaneously throughout the day. I even knew what color my eyes are.

What finally got me out of my depression was learning what loving myself really meant. I didn't understand I deserved to be happy. I thought I was meant to be sad, and so I remained sad. But that's not how you treat someone you love. You're not okay when they're sad. You work hard to make them happy. Once I started doing that, I started to rebuild my life.

Overcoming my depression introduced me to the concept of loving myself, but it was during a relapse that I truly learned *how* to love myself. For anyone who's suffered from depression, you know it's not something that ever completely goes away. There will be moments, days, and even weeks where you relapse and feel like you're back at square one. When I experienced these episodes, I had to treat myself with extra love and care. I didn't want to go back to a place of depression, so I became my own best friend. I did this in a few ways:

1 I WASN'T SO HARD ON MYSELF. I would reassure myself that a relapse didn't mean I was weak or unworthy or that I deserved to be sad. It was simply a bad feeling that would pass.

2 I ENCOURAGED MYSELF, sometimes even out loud. I would tell myself that I was strong and that no bad day could ruin all the beautiful things going on in life.

3 **I WAS PATIENT WITH MYSELF** and understood that if I needed to feel sad for a while, that was okay. Whether I was sad or happy or scared, I was there for myself, hugging myself, and being proud of whatever emotion I felt.

I don't often relapse these days (#blessed), but regardless, I'm still completely in love with myself and consider myself my own best friend. Even now, when I'm having a bad day, I will talk to myself with empathy. I'll say things like, "All right, today was rough and you're feeling crappy. But you made it through and that's good on you. Give yourself a hug and make tomorrow a better day." When I achieve things I'm proud of, I literally pat myself on the back and say, "I am so damn proud of you, Lilly!" That may sound weird, but it shouldn't. When you love someone, you communicate with them openly.

When we're dealing with difficult situations we tend to think about how our actions will affect others. If I make this decision, how will my mom feel? How will my husband feel? How will it affect my brother? Will anyone be mad? It's great to consider other people's feelings, but don't forget that you're also a person who deserves to be considered. It's essential for you to stop and think about how something makes YOU feel. Then you can make a decision based on EVERYONE you love. That's the difference between being selfish and loving yourself.

I used to be so scared to spend time alone. Now I love being by myself sometimes. Like any other relationship, the one you have with yourself takes time and effort. Don't bully yourself into thinking you don't deserve to be loved. That's ridiculous! You should walk up to a mirror and serenade yourself right now. May I suggest Beyoncé's "Crazy in Love"? Because that's how you should feel about your reflection.

66 LIKE ANY OTHER RELATIONSHIP, THE ONE YOU HAVE WITH YOURSELF TAKES TIME AND EFFORT.

You will not work hard for yourself if you don't love yourself. You will not fulfill your dreams if you dislike the person who dreamed them. If you want to be a Bawse, give yourself a hug and mean it.

Write a Love Song

List five things you love about yourself. And don't be superficial—
no hair, eyes, or legs BS! Get real with yourself.

1. _____

_____

2. _____

_____

3. _____

_____

4. _____

_____

5. _____

_____

CHAPTER 12

PAUSE

PEOPLE OFTEN ASK

me if I have a clone—how do I manage to get so much done? A true Bawse is able to get a LOT done in one day, and as a result, people can't help but wonder, "Do they sleep?" I get that question a lot. The answer is yes, I sleep. I love sleep. But when I'm awake, I'm awake 2.0. That means I treat my waking hours like I'm making up for the time I've spent asleep. I want to do so much in a day that when my head hits my pillow at night, I'm exhausted and feel I've earned the right to catch some z's. Many people I admire all share this quality, this relentless work ethic that allows them to complete tasks back to back throughout their day. My friends always joke that they need to pretend to be doing work around me in order to keep up. I'm not telling you this to brag (although, heyyyy); I'm telling you because I'm now going to let you in on what keeps me going. The key to hustling hard is to pause.

You can only work relentlessly on something if you ENJOY doing it. If I hated Superwoman and everything she entailed, there's no way I could wake up, check forty emails, write a script, attend a meeting, check thirty more emails, record a video, edit the video, do a conference call, release the video, do an interview, and also vlog throughout it all. It's a bit easier to bear a nine-to-five job that you hate because you know that at 5:00 P.M. you're checking out, speeding away in your car while giving the middle finger in your rearview mirror. But if you have a career or goal that consumes your entire day, you need to like it to succeed. Enjoying what you do is the only way you can commit so much time and energy to your work. But let's be real, no matter how much you enjoy something, it can still wear you down. So how do you stay in love with your work? How do you wake up next to it every morning and still feel excited about how sexy it is? You pause. You can only enjoy something if you take a moment to appreciate it and pay attention to it. That's why you slowly take the first bite of your dessert instead of gobbling up the entire thing. You savor it.

When you're a Bawse and hustling every day, life can seem like it's speeding past you. Decisions need to be made TODAY, you have ten urgent emails that need to be answered RIGHT NOW, three people need you to call them ASAP, and you have two deadlines for TONIGHT. Your days, weeks, and months—your whole life—can start seeming like a blur, and you're just trying to see straight. I've learned that I thrive with this kind of schedule (or at least that's what I've convinced myself). I am like the Energizer bunny: I never think I'll burn out. But I did once, and that's when I learned the importance of pausing.

I was attending a camp in Italy with some really cool people, and I was totally star-struck. One of those people was Pharrell Williams, and I would be lying if I said I didn't internally fangirl while meeting him. When I arrived in Italy I was very tired, hoping to relax and sleep in. Prior to this trip I'd been in L.A. for two hours to pack, gone to Montreal to accept an award, done a fifteen-hour music video shoot, and attended a movie pre-miere after a morning of doing press, all while participating in meetings and making my weekly videos. When I arrived in Italy, I sat on my hotel bed and opened my itinerary with excitement. The first thing I saw was "Day starts at 8:00 A.M.," and I instantly went numb. 8:00 A.M.? Why? WHY 8:00 A.M.? WHY NOT PASTA AND COCKTAILS AT A SOLID 2:00 P.M. BY THE POOL?! Or 1:45 if you're feeling professional.

The next morning I woke up and started the day at 8:00 A.M., feeling completely indifferent about my day ahead, despite the fact that I was in this amazing place with amazing people. I felt numb while I ate break-fast and felt even more numb at the first event I attended. But it wasn't until my conversation with Pharrell that I knew I was totally burned out and needed some down time. There I was, in Italy, on the way to an ancient temple to have dinner under the stars, and sitting in front of Phar-rell Williams, who was telling me all about his life experiences, and the only thought I had was, "I can't wait to go to sleep." How ridiculous and ungrateful a thought! That's the result of going and going and going and not giving yourself a moment to pause and reflect on why you're even going in the first place. The reason I "go" is because I crave amazing life experi-ences. My most prized accomplishments have nothing to do with money or status and everything to do with meeting cool people and experiencing unique things in different places around the world. Yet there I was, having an amazing experience but yearning for my bed. What a sad thing it is to work so hard and yet be unable to enjoy the fruits of your labor.

Since that camp, I have become a lot better at pausing and reflecting. Here are a couple ways I do it:

1 MEDITATE

Whenever I tell people I meditate, they assume I wake up at 5:00 A.M. every day, put my legs behind my head, recite hymns, and bathe with flowers. No. Five in the morning? Are you kidding me? That's when I sleep. Also, if I could put my legs behind my head, well, my love life would be a lot different. I don't know how to meditate in accordance with any textbook, religion, or culture, nor do I do it every day. I've made up my own version of meditation that works for me, and I encourage you to do the same. I do it when I'm feeling stressed, tired, upset, or ungrateful, or when I have any other negative emotion that I'm trying to defuse.

Here's what I do: I sit on the floor, cross-legged, in a quiet place. I find somewhere that is away from any noise or other people, somewhere shut off, like a closet or small bedroom. I light a candle and place it on the floor in front of me. I use a candle labeled "positive energy," but I can't say for sure that it really does anything. (I'm easily sold by wonderful marketing. There's no shame in my game.) With my eyes closed, I take a few deep breaths and slowly smile as genuinely as I possibly can. I'm not smiling for a camera or for someone else, but because I'm alone and I can be alone

"
DON'T CHEAT
YOURSELF
BY BLAZING
THROUGH
YOUR LIFE.
"

with my smile. Then I whisper things to myself. I talk about what's bothering me, what I want to achieve, how I want my day to go, what I want to improve, or what I'm scared of. Whatever I end up saying, I always end my meditation practice in the same way: I remind myself of all the amazing things I have AND that I am my own best advocate.

Why do I do this? One, because it genuinely calms me down and makes me feel better, and two, because in a day that's so go-go-go, I want to pay attention to my feelings and not just dismiss them. If I'm feeling upset, I deserve to take a few moments for myself. I'm pausing so I can remember that I enjoy the experience of hustling, which therefore allows me to continue hustling. There have been many times when I've felt the need to meditate but my schedule didn't allow for it. When that happens, I kindly request a fifteen-minute pause so I can get my energy in the right place. That's not selfish. That pause is beneficial to me and everyone else who is relying on me to be efficient and productive.

2 DISCONNECT

It used to be that when people would accomplish something amazing, they would enjoy the moment and celebrate with friends and family. Today when you accomplish something great, it's a failure unless you capture it on Snapchat (bonus points if you're using the puppy filter!). That's wack. As someone who has a career built around social media, I love capturing big moments and I encourage you to do so as well. BUT not at the expense of enjoying the moment in real time. When you are experiencing something exciting, beautiful, or rewarding, try to disconnect and just take the moment in. For example, when you go to a concert, as soon as the lights go down, everyone pulls out their phone. Why? You have three hours to take a picture or capture a video; why would you choose this very first moment to do so? Why not embrace the moment? View it through your own eyes instead of a screen. Then, during a slow song, when your panties are in less of a bunch, take a picture and satisfy that craving.

Now, when I experience something amazing, I pause and try to be in the moment. During my last trip to Singapore, I was alone, sitting by the famous Marina Bay Sands infinity pool, which is essentially a giant floating pool high up in the sky. I took a picture, vlogged a little, and then put all my electronics away. I climbed into the pool, positioned myself at the edge, and spent twenty minutes staring out at the cityscape, admiring its beauty. During those twenty minutes I thanked God for the opportunity, I looked at each building, I appreciated the cuteness of the family swimming to the right of me, I thought about my incredible career, and I felt the water against my skin. In that moment, I was totally present. I was nowhere else except that pool. That twenty-minute pause gave me the fuel I needed to keep going in the weeks to come.

When I meet people I admire, I take ten minutes out of my day to think about the meeting, smile about it, and fangirl. If I win an award, I will go through the rounds of speeches, media, and celebrations, but then I will sit by myself and hold the trophy for a few minutes in silence. If I want to continue working as hard as possible, I need to FEEL and truly EXPE-RIENCE the fruits of my labor. Inspiration fuels the hustle, and what better inspiration than enjoying the results of your hard work? Don't cheat yourself by blazing through your life. Reflection is necessary and should be on your to-do list.

Life is like one giant YouTube video: it's amazing to experience, but when too many things are happening at once, you begin to lag. You try waiting it out, but sure enough, the lagging just gets worse and worse. Now you're just frozen. You are Elsa. That's not enjoyable for anyone, especially not you. So what do you do? Pause the video and regroup. Once you've had a moment to load up, press play again, and see how much your quality has improved. That pause in your life is your responsibility. So press pause every once in a while and savor the moment.

OUT OF THE BLUE

2009 I hate this feeling. I hate it so much because it doesn't even feel like a feeling anymore; it just feels like who I am. I'm this broken human sitting on the floor in her basement. At this same moment, other people are probably having dinner, traveling with their loved ones, reading a great book, or laughing with their best friends. I bet they're all doing something amazing. But not me. Instead I'm curled up in a ball, leaning against the bar in my basement, with my face in my hands. I can't stop crying. I can't control my breathing. I'm powerless against the whirlwind of negative thoughts and angry voices that are constantly assaulting me.

Why have people hurt me? Why do people lie? Am I so worthless that people feel they can easily dismiss me? Am I that insignificant a human being? I don't get it. I have been through so many heartaches in life and I've always persevered. But this time is different. After years of standing tall in my corner, life has landed the final punch to my chest and I've gone tumbling down. I don't know how to get back up. And, truthfully, I don't know if my life is worth getting back up for. How did I get here? Growing up, I had high hopes for myself. I was an imaginative kid who had crazy dreams of becoming a rapper, hanging out with The Rock, and traveling the world. But today I have none of that. I've been robbed of my confidence, strength, and imagination.

I take a huge gulp of whiskey that is now seasoned with my pathetic tears. It burns my throat and I practically gag from the horrible, unfamiliar taste. I don't drink. I've never had a desire to drink alcohol. Yet here I am, drinking alone, just hoping that I'll be able to fall asleep soon. I am so disgusted with my situation that I start insulting myself out loud. I raise my glass. "Cheers to you, Lilly. Cheers for being the most pathetic person you know. Cheers to being that idiot everyone lies to. A big cheers for ever thinking you were someone special. I hope you know better than that now. And finally, cheers to another horrible night." I've hit rock bottom.

2015

My hand is shaking as I hold my glass up. I'm in my hotel room with my team. I cannot stop the whirlwind of exhilarating thoughts. We clink glasses. "Cheers! We're going to the MTV Movie Awards!"

Last night I mustered up all my courage and messaged my childhood hero, Dwayne "The Rock" Johnson, because I knew he'd be attending the event. We've recently become text friends, but I haven't yet met him. I'm so nervous I couldn't sleep at all last night. Fast-forward to today. I'm FREAKING OUT.

I look in the mirror. I smile as I look into my own eyes. How is this my life? How did I manage to pick myself up from the darkest time in my life? I'm so proud of myself.

I'm in my seat sipping champagne as I try to take it all in. The room is full of celebrities I admire, magnificent set pieces, and glamorous outfits. Oh, and hey, that's Zac Efron. God, he's hot. *ping* Wait, did he just say "ping"?! No. Wait. That was my phone. I just received a text: *Lilly, come to the greenroom. He's here.*

I AM NOT OKAY. I enter the greenroom and see Dwayne from across the room. My knees begin to shake. Maybe this is a joke?! But then . . . Dwayne turns and notices me. He interrupts the man he's speaking to and says, "Hey, sorry, give me a second. I've got to meet someone really important."

Dwayne gives me a big hug and a kiss on the cheek. He knows my name. He knows about my tour. He knows my catchphrases. He says he's *my* fan.

I get back to my hotel room and sit on my bed. I'm so overwhelmed that I start talking to myself out loud: "You deserve this, Lilly. Keep going and don't you dare stop now." Suddenly tears are streaming down my face. I can't stop crying. But now they are tears of happiness. I can't believe I get to meet the man who delivers "The Rock Bottom."

PART 2
HUSTLE
HARDER

Now that you and your mind are BFFs, you can work together to focus on your goals. In this section you will learn best practices for getting work done, getting rid of distractions, staying organized, and creating meaningful success. Be fore-warned that success isn't easily obtained. If you want to be a Bawse, you'll need to hustle. And then hustle harder.

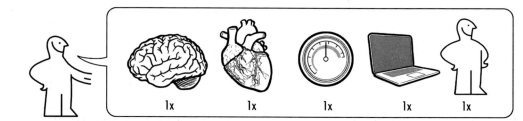

1x   1x   1x   1x   1x

CHAPTER 13

COMMIT

TO YOUR

ECISIONS

GOOD COMMITMENTS

are like endangered animals—there are many threats to their existence. You make a New Year's resolution to work out every day and promise yourself it'll happen. The next day you wake up bright and early, go to the gym, and feel great about your new responsible lifestyle. Look at you—you're basically a fitness guru and will likely only eat kale from this point on. The next day you wake up early again and go to the gym, thus solidifying your future spot in the Olympics. The next day, however, you can't seem to stop hitting the snooze button and sleep in, missing your only gym opportunity for the day. The morning after that, you wake up with a sore throat and stay in bed. Your commitment is on a battlefield, and sleep and sickness are charging toward it holding spears. Not far behind those threats are parties, laziness, Instagram, and Netflix. Your favorite TV show ending on a cliffhanger is added ammunition. What am I getting at? Committing to your decisions is extremely difficult work. And also, stop trying to make kale a thing!

Being a Bawse requires you not only to make great decisions that will help you achieve your goals but also to commit to those decisions regardless of the obstacles you will face. The two most common obstacles are usually fear and distraction. Let's say you decide to start a daily blog. Fear will convince you that your writing isn't good enough and, as a result, people will judge you harshly. Do you really want to fail and be made fun of? Distractions, such as parties, will convince you that your time would be better spent doing something other than working on your blog. After all, it's an open bar and you're cheap! What you need to remember is that when you make a commitment, there is no asterisk at the bottom stating that the decision is valid until obstacles are present. Your commitment isn't a coupon with fine print.

A couple of years ago I had the opportunity to shoot a collaboration video with Seth Rogen and James Franco as a promotion for their upcoming movie, *The Interview.* I was thrilled about the opportunity and flew to L.A. to make it happen, as I was living in Toronto at the time. I was determined to ace this collab, so I even flew out my videographer, Rick, just to ensure that everything went smoothly. We built an entire set, memorized our creative shot by shot, and rehearsed the workflow over and over again. This was because—plot twist—we had only forty-five minutes to shoot with the boys. The forty-five minutes included the time it would take them to walk into the building, meet us, and listen to our creative. Forty-five minutes to shoot a nine-minute skit is NOT a lot of time, especially when I need to play three different characters. Despite the enormousness of the task ahead of us, Rick and I committed to shooting the video in the allotted time and promised ourselves that nothing would get in the way of that. We were like your iPhone in the morning: charged up.

I'll never forget when Seth and James walked into the room because it was one of the rare times in my life when I was so busy that I'd forgotten to be nervous ahead of time. I'd been so preoccupied preparing and rehearsing that I'd completely overlooked the fact that I would be starstruck. When they walked in, the feeling hit me like a brick wall and my stomach instantly tied itself into a knot. Say hello to obstacle number one: nerves. OMG, it's Seth Rogen and James effing Franco!

I shook it off and began to confidently explain my creative to the boys as quickly as possible because I knew the clock was ticking. As I shared my jokes with them, I saw a bit of confusion on James's face. Therein entered obstacle number two: fear. *What if I'm not funny and they hate this? Am I in the wrong career? OMG, OMG! Am I ugly? I'm ugly, aren't I? UGH, damn it. I'm Shrek.*

Once again I shook it off and carried on at lightning speed. We were blowing through all our shoots as planned and I was feeling a burst of adrenaline. Things were going great until, midway through the shoot, the ten people on set began talking, louder and louder. I was in the center of the room trying to recite dialogue while in the background I could hear conversations and the sound of a camera clicking as the producers tried to capture behind-the-scenes footage. Cue obstacle number three: distractions. Aside from being distracting, all this commotion was also interfering with the sound quality of my video, and so I began to get stressed.

Guess what I did? I shook it off like a salt shaker and kept on cruising with determination. One part of the skit required me to kiss Seth Rogen while dressed as my mother, because why not. So without hesitation and with time restraints in mind, I leaned in and laid one on him, feeling proud of my confidence. Now, if you know anything about Seth, you know he openly enjoys participating in certain leisure activities that involve an altered state of mind, particularly ones that involve green leaves . . . rolled up . . . and lit on fire (yes, kids, I'm talking about spinach). After kissing Seth once, I felt a sensation I wasn't familiar with. I had a strange taste in my mouth and a strong scent on my lips. We had to reshoot the scene three more times to capture different camera angles, and with each kiss I felt more and more strange. Welcome, obstacle number four: foreign substances. Wait, is that a pink unicorn? Eating a pizza? Under a rainbow?! WHEN DID I START FLOATING?!

Okay, I'm exaggerating. Aside from me, there were no unicorns in the room, but I swear I felt a little weird and light-headed! After an intense forty-five minutes, I'd shot my video, and the boys exited just as fast as they'd entered. I collapsed onto a sofa and instantly reflected on the shoot. I recognized that it had indeed been a challenging situation, but I was proud that I'd honored my commitment to get it done, regardless of the obstacles. I didn't slow my pace down because of nerves, alter my jokes because of fear, forget my dialogue because of distractions, or stop kissing a man because he smelled like Snoop Dogg. As a reminder, before the shoot started, I'd said I was going to "shoot the video in forty-five minutes." I didn't say "I am going to shoot the video in forty-five minutes unless I get nervous or scared or distracted." What kind of commitment would that be? A lame one. You shouldn't make lame commitments. Leave that for the politicians.

You'll never truly know if you can accomplish something or be great at something if you don't commit. In other words, if you've ever tried 70 percent at something and failed, you didn't give yourself a fair chance at success. You crippled yourself in your own race.

Now, at this point you should be yelling at the page, saying, "Hey, Shrek! That's easier said than done! How do you control fear and nerves?" In response, I have two things to say:

1 **FIRST, I THINK IT'S IMPORTANT TO NOTE** that fear and nervousness are things you shouldn't be afraid to experience. I'll be full of regret the day I ever go onstage, shoot a movie, or meet someone iconic without feeling scared or nervous. Being scared and nervous means you care, and not only is caring a beautiful thing, but it also means you value the outcome of a situation. However, fear and nervousness become problematic when they affect your performance. Understanding when to adopt and abandon these feelings is an important first step in controlling them. It's helpful to think of fear and nerves as an outfit you wear before doing something nerve-racking. Don't try to avoid these feelings altogether; rather, get comfortable with taking the outfit off when it's time to execute. I am grateful to be in a place where I am extremely nervous before I go on, but once my foot hits that stage, I'm fearless. Nerves might make me pee forty times before a performance, but I try my best to put a leash on that emotion once the show starts. I envision myself stripping away a layer of fear and uncovering the complete fearlessness below. Literally, I go through the motions of taking off an imaginary jacket made of fear. This motion also doubles as the Macarena, so congrats, you're now a dancer.

2 **BEFORE DOING ANYTHING THAT IS NERVE-RACKING** or scary, such as going onstage, doing a TV appearance, walking into an audition, making a presentation, or meeting an idol, I perform a very specific routine. I kick everyone out of the room, escape through the window, and run away as fast as possible. Just kidding! Please, I would never voluntarily run. But what I do instead is have a conversation with myself in the mirror. Aside from beating my chest, pumping myself up, and humming the *Rocky* theme music, I say something very specific: "Fear and nervousness are nowhere on the path to success." I then hold up my left index finger and say, "You are here right now." I lift my right index finger, hold it apart from the left one, and say, "This is the goal." When I look at my reflection in the mirror, I can see that the space between my two fingers is filled with nothing but air. There is no fear, nervousness, or distraction in that space. I suggest you try this the next time you have to do something scary, because most of the obstacles we face are the ones we make up in our minds. Just make sure you're alone, or someone might throw a straitjacket on you, and it's hard to eat pizza in those things.

To be a Bawse, you need to get down on one knee, propose to your decisions, and commit to them for a lifetime. That's what your decisions deserve—100 percent. Not 90 percent, 80 percent, or, like your iPhone twenty minutes after you wake up, 30 percent. It's all or nothing, baby!

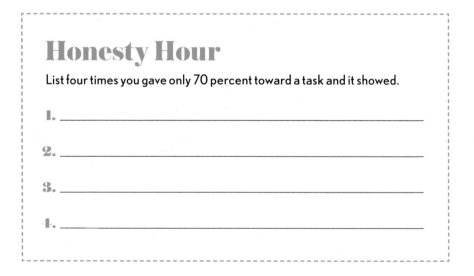

Honesty Hour

List four times you gave only 70 percent toward a task and it showed.

1. _____

2. _____

3. _____

4. _____

"

YOU'LL NEVER TRULY KNOW IF YOU CAN **ACCOMPLISH SOMETHING** OR BE GREAT AT **SOMETHING** IF YOU DON'T **COMMIT.**

"

CHAPTER 14

LET GO
OF
FOMO

IF I HAD A DOLLAR

for every time I was tempted to hang out with my friends instead of doing work, I'd have a yacht made of gold. In fact, I'd be so rich that my yacht would have a yacht for when it wants to take a break. That's right. I'd be so rich that my yacht would be a human with needs. #YachtGoals

The point is, I get it and I've been there. You have work to do and your friends are all going out, about to have the time of their lives. You'll be at your desk reviewing documents and they'll probably be out winning the lottery and taking cute pictures with perfect lighting; to be honest, they'll probably run into Katy Perry and do fireworks together. Or at least that's what your brain is convincing you will happen. Do you hear that? It's FOMO knocking on your door.

For all you unhip elderly folk who don't know what FOMO is, get with the times! In other words, Google it like I did and pretend you knew the meaning all along. Duh. FOMO is the *fear of missing out,* and it's a crucial obstacle to overcome on the road to success. FOMO is not only strong enough to encourage you to stop working but also sly enough to convince you that you've got your priorities all wrong. It's that voice that says, "You're going to miss out on life for a good grade? That's stupid! School is a ridiculous institution. Maybe you shouldn't believe in the system! YEAH! EFF THE SYSTEM." The next thing you know you're wearing a tie-dye shirt and using words like "rad," all because you wanted to go to the movies instead of write an essay.

Temptations to slack off will always be there, and that will never change. What has to change is your ability to deal with temptation. To be successful, you need to be able to look FOMO in the eyes and say NO. In response, FOMO will stand there, pout, and throw a temper tantrum, but you have to be strong and hold your ground. The only way to overcome FOMO is to recognize that the joy of accomplishing goals is much greater than the disappointment of missing out on a little fun. Parties are fun in the short term, but fulfilling your goals will bring you greater happiness in the long term. Also, there's probably a line to use the bathroom at the party, and who the hell wants to hold in their pee only to hover over a disgusting toilet seat? Eff that. You'd rather get some work done. Plus, no one can hold the hover for that long. LET'S BE REAL.

If we're honest, though, that's easy to say and hard to do. I know this because I had my biggest battle with FOMO in quite a surreal setting. Let me paint you a picture. Midway through my world tour, YouTube flew my dancers and me out to L.A. so I could continue working on my show and work on their marketing campaign at the same time. Eleven of my friends and I stayed in a Hollywood Hills mansion stocked with junk food, alcohol, a pool table, and a shuffleboard court, along with a stunning view. It was like a reality show, except with values and morals.

The YouTube campaign was one that would put my face on billboards, streetcars, taxicabs, and bus shelters, and even in Times Square. New York! I had been waiting ages to be selected for this, especially since the deal had fallen through the year before. Needless to say, I was excited about this accomplishment, and my panties were in several knots. The campaign required a few days of shooting during which I had to get up at ungodly hours of the morning. Apparently there's a time called 6:00 A.M.? Riding the high of my excitement and gratitude, I was happy to sacrifice my love of sleep—that is, until . . .

> 'Twas the night before shooting, and all through the house,
> Vodka and soda were stirring, mixed drinks to the mouth.
> My friends all having fun, that's what I could hear—
> Music blasting, girls laughing, the sound of their cheers.
> I was still awake, all stressed in my bed
> As visions of FOMO danced in my head . . .

Okay, I have to stop there because I don't actually know the rest of that poem. I think Santa eventually shows up, but honestly, it could be a cliffhanger where the kids are actually Jewish and Santa is a lie.

Anyway, there I was, lying in bed at 10:00 P.M. trying to be responsible and resting for my 6:00 A.M. wake-up call, and all I could hear were the sounds of pure joy below me. It sounded like my friends were having the best night of their entire lives. Music. Dancing. Jokes. Maybe even a bear, I'm not sure. *OMG. If Winnie the Pooh is here partying with them THIS ONE TIME I HAVE TO GO TO SLEEP EARLY, I'm going to be so pissed.*

In the moment, my brain was convincing me that this party was the be-all and end-all of all parties and that my decision to go to sleep early was preposterous. I remember lying there reevaluating my entire life and thinking, "Is this the type of career you want? You're missing this once-in-a-lifetime fun for work? And probably your only chance of ever meeting Winnie?"

I had two options: (1) rip off my blanket, speed down the stairs doing the running man, and grab two beers to catch up, or (2) shut up, close my eyes, and go to sleep so I could perform well the next day. I'm proud to say I chose the latter. But it wasn't easy. I put a pillow over my face and forced myself to go to sleep while envisioning myself on a billboard in Times Square. My FOMO was conquered for one night, but I still had two nights to go. FOMO is like that annoying computer update that you ignore but it comes back the next night trying to get your attention all over again. It's a constant test, and it's one every Bawse needs to learn how to pass.

How? Train your brain to pay attention to the rewards you receive when hustle beats FOMO on the battlefield. Fast-forward six months and I'm standing in Times Square with my family, taking pictures in front of my billboard. My face is painted on the side of a building in Manhattan. A

bus just passed by and my goofy grin is plastered all over it. Do you think for even a second that I stood there in New York City, watching tourists take pictures with my face as a backdrop and thought, "Damn, I wish I didn't miss that little party that one night"? No. The answer is no.

So pay close attention to the good grade you got when you studied instead of partied. Don't just let that moment pass. Really take it in and think about how it makes you feel. Think about the promotion you got for staying late instead of going for drinks with your co-workers. Make a list of your accomplishments and recognize how you achieved them. Focusing on your work moves you closer to reaching your goals. That is a fact. Keep training your brain to pay attention to how rewarding it is to work hard. Soon you'll stop worrying about what parties you missed, and you'll develop a hustler's FOMO: the fear of missing out on accomplishment.

So the next time you're faced with FOMO (and I promise you, there will be a next time), ask yourself one question: "What will my future self thank me for doing today?" Once you answer that question, shut up, work hard, and go accomplish your goals.

Also, I learned that Winnie wasn't there and I didn't hear a bear. One of my friends just coughed and sneezed at the same time. Oh, FOMO, you're so silly.

Attack FOMO

List three accomplishments that were a result of your hard work.

1. _____ (TAKE THAT, FOMO)

2. _____ (BOOM)

3. _____ (MIC DROP)

CHAPTER 15

SCHEDULE INSPIRATION

I WOULD NEED

more than two hands to count the number of times I've been in the middle of a commute on the highway and stressing out because my gas light is on. It's a super-huge first-world problem, I know, but filling up my tank is one of the most annoying parts of my week. Chances are I'm running late and this pit stop will make me EVEN later. And if it's winter, I might as well just say goodbye to the functionality of my fingers. True pain is pulling up at a gas station in winter and realizing you don't have gloves. And I'm not talking about a cute little Los Angeles winter; I'm talking about a real, ruthless Toronto winter. It feels like you're shaking hands with Olaf, but he doesn't let go for five whole minutes. But you have no choice because you need gas to get from one destination to another.

Inspiration is the fuel for your hustle. It runs through our inner engine and gives us the drive (see what I did there?) to get from our starting point to the accomplishment of our goals. Just like a car, when you're running low on inspiration you need to refuel to get to your final destination.

No matter how much you love doing something and how happy it makes you, you're human and you will have moments when you're feeling unmotivated. I love making videos and I am grateful every day to have the career I have, but some Mondays I'll wake up and I'd rather put my hair in a blender than make a video. The thought of writing a script, setting up my camera on my broken tripod, pretending I know how to use my lights, recording myself, editing the footage, and waiting for a video to upload makes me want to curl up into a fetal position and cry. And that's okay. A Bawse knows that a lack of motivation doesn't equal failure, nor is it a permanent weakness. A Bawse expects it and addresses it.

Often we think about inspiration as something that just hits us suddenly. Maybe we overheard a great conversation, won tickets to a great musical, or met someone new with a fresh perspective—something that ignited (or reignited) a spark within us. Spontaneous inspiration is one of the greatest surprises that can happen in your day, but if it doesn't, don't be discouraged. I've become a big believer in scheduling inspiration. For me, that means proactively orchestrating events that will help make me feel inspired. I don't want my hustle to rely solely on spontaneous events, so I take matters into my own hands.

My daily to-do list includes items like:

- Clear inbox
- Read movie script
- Conference call
- Make video
- Send creative pitch

And then at the very end of the list will be a shining gem that says:

- Watch *The Walking Dead*

Anyone who's known me for a while might laugh at that because I'm always the one to say, "I don't have time to watch shows, I'm too busy creating my own." It's true, I am busy creating my own content, but watching shows and movies has become part of my work (#blessedlife). I discovered their value last year when I had my wisdom teeth removed. Like most people, I was a useless chipmunk, high on painkillers, trying to distract myself from the hell that was my current life. I took the opportunity to finally listen to my friends and Twitter (same thing?) and started watching *Game of Thrones*. It was a strange idea to me, to sit in one place for several hours and mindlessly stare at a show on a screen, but I did it to ease my pain. In exactly sixty minutes, I was hooked. The story line was one I'd never encountered before, the costumes and set design were so extravagant, and the dialogue made me want to shed tears of joy. Want to see a grown woman cry? Let Emilia Clarke drop a one-liner about girl power.

Watching *Game of Thrones* inspired me to think about my own content differently. Suddenly I had new ideas, I was paying more attention to one-liners in my own script, and I was increasing the production value of my shoots. Watching the show wasn't JUST helping me relax—it was also helping me become better at my craft.

Once I flew through all the seasons, like most of the population, I had major *Game of Thrones* withdrawal. That's when I decided to fill the void with *The Walking Dead*. I thought, "There's no way a show about zombies could inspire me the way *Game of Thrones* did. I've seen a million zombie movies." To my surprise, I was completely wrong. *The Walking Dead* inspired me in a completely different way, with unique character development, plot twists, and tension that provoked extreme anxiety in me. Watching this show not only got the wheels spinning in my creative mind but created brand-new wheels that hadn't been there before.

INSPIRATION IS THE FUEL FOR YOUR HUSTLE.

After *The Walking Dead* came *Stranger Things* and, well, I watched that in two days. In my defense, as of the time I'm writing this, there's only one season! Don't judge me too harshly. As expected, *Stranger Things* inspired me to start thinking about sci-fi themes and supernatural abilities. I immediately wanted to feature more children in my videos because apparently they're all more talented than me. And if these shows didn't directly inspire me to think about content differently, they definitely inspired my jokes. While I was watching these shows, I'd reference them constantly in my videos, and my audience LOVED it. They enjoyed knowing that I was as invested in the characters as they were and, more than anything, they loved knowing that we both watched the same shows. It's made my content that much more relatable.

In addition to watching shows, I also schedule inspiration by taking breaks from my work and using that time to watch interviews of people I admire. If I'm struggling to write a comedy script, I'll watch an interview with Rebel Wilson or Amy Schumer. If I'm struggling to write lyrics, I'll watch an interview with Nicki Minaj or Drake. I think there's something so inspirational about hearing about other people's experiences and what drives them. It's almost like they're lending you some of their fuel or giving you a boost with spiritual jumper cables. Hearing someone so accomplished talk about their struggles and successes has definitely become crucial inspirational fuel for me. Therefore, I make time to watch a decent number of interviews every week. It's my version of taking a break in a meaningful way—a productive break, if you will.

Sometimes we go too long with our gas light on and our car stops in the middle of the road. Everyone is honking at you and you're just staring straight ahead in complete frustration, pretending not to hear them.

HELLO, I AM NOT HERE BY CHOICE. It's not impossible to get your car going again, but it'll definitely take some more work. You'll have to call a tow truck or walk to the nearest gas station, buy an overpriced gas container, fill it up, and walk back to your car.

You can expect the same to happen when you've been hustling for a long time without refueling. While I was planning my first tour, I spent every waking moment working on the creative for a good few weeks. One evening I caught myself feeling dead inside and I knew my hustle had halted on the side of the road. People were honking at me. And by people, I mean my production team, who were waiting for my final show script. I got up and walked away from my work. I headed straight to my room and zoned out for a bit. That night I was supposed to go out with a few friends and my brain was dreading it, since I was already so completely drained of energy. I couldn't bear the thought of having to be social. Instead, I canceled my plans and spent the night watching the Beyoncé documentary. As I sat there alone, it was like Beyoncé was speaking to me, because so much of what she was saying was what I was feeling at the time (and also because I wish she was my BFF). In tears, I watched as Queen Bey gave me all the wisdom and knowledge I needed. Through her story, I could feel my needle moving from empty to full. The next morning, I woke up with new purpose and a reignited desire to work on my tour. Lemonade was flowing through my veins.

When you're sick, you get into bed and allow yourself to heal. When your hustle is not feeling well, you should prescribe it some inspiration and do the same. I canceled my plans that night because my hustle needed healing. Here are a few suggestions for what to watch to jump-start your inspiration:

- The documentary *Justin Bieber: Never Say Never*
- The documentary *Katy Perry: Part of Me*
- The documentary *Beyoncé: Life Is But a Dream*
- *A Trip to Unicorn Island,* by yours truly *innocent smile*

Having said all of this, I now drive an electric car, so I don't deal with the nuisance of getting gas. I don't need to refuel my car, just my hustle, and I take that task very seriously. All I have to do now is remember to plug in my car and . . . crap.

HOOOOOOOOONNNNKKKKKK.

CHAPTER 16

HAVE VISIONS

WHAT IF EVERY DAY

were Christmas and you could ask Santa for whatever you wanted in life? Sometimes you'd get what you asked for because you were nice, but other times you wouldn't because you were a naughty brat. Well, life is kind of like that except that every day isn't Christmas; it's an opportunity to hustle. And Santa doesn't exist (I was paid off to say this! Keep believing, kids!), but you can still get what you ask for if you work hard enough. Every day you can close your eyes and imagine all the things you want. A Bawse doesn't just know what they want for Christmas; they know what they want from life. They have visions.

Don't get weirded out. I'm not going to get all sci-fi on you. And I won't tell you to have visions about the future and predict horrific tragedies because the last thing we need is another *Final Destination* movie. We get it. You can't escape death. Just like we can't escape that story line. However, I am going to explain the importance of two types of visions: vision boards and visualization.

I'm sure this is not the first time you've heard of a vision board. That's because it's not a concept I made up. It's a pretty well-known device that most people know from the book and film *The Secret*. If you have no idea what I'm talking about, then yes, I invented vision boards.

A vision board is a piece of paper, a piece of Bristol board, or a chalkboard—any surface, really—that has images of all the things you want to obtain in life. The idea is to collect images that represent your goals and paste them onto the board to create a collage. Then you place the board someplace where you will see it often, reminding you of your goals. I've made two vision boards so far in my life and can tell you firsthand that they have positively impacted my hustle and my mind. Here are three reasons you should have a vision board:

" A BAWSE DOESN'T JUST KNOW WHAT THEY WANT FOR CHRISTMAS; THEY KNOW WHAT THEY WANT FROM LIFE.

1 Creating a vision board gives you clarity about what your goals are. People know they have to work really hard, so they do, but sometimes they're unsure of what they're really working for. What's the goal? After all, you can't get what you want in life if you don't know what you want. Not having a clear understanding of what your goals are is like not putting an address into a GPS before driving. Something like "money" isn't a clear goal. How will you ever know if you've made enough money to achieve your goal of making money? Does money mean a nice tux or a private jet? Set clear goals and define them with clear images. You can't hustle toward a blurry picture because you'll never know if you've gotten there. Create a vision board and be honest about what you want. If you want a nice car, put it on there. If you want a six-pack, put it on there. If you want to travel the world, put it on there too. If you want to date Channing Tatum, same—but that might not work. Everything else, though, PUT IT ON THERE! Now you know what you're aiming for.

2 Creating a vision board helps you to be self-aware, which, it goes without saying, is a key Bawse quality. Success is subjective. For some people, success means owning a yacht; for others, it means being a good parent; for still others, it means running a 10K marathon. When you begin pasting your goals onto a board, you can have a better understanding of how you define success. Your vision board will be filled with all the things you think are important—and what you think is important is very telling. Taking a look at your vision board can often help you understand why you make the decisions you make. If you're unsure why you love to work late nights at the office even though your fiancé hates it, the picture of a CEO's desk on your vision board might be the answer. Or maybe it's the picture of a stack of money.

3 A vision board allows you to be constantly reminded of what you want in life. Now that you've gained clarity and self-awareness, you can motivate yourself by storing your goals in your subconscious. What better way to do that than to stare at images of your goals? I keep my vision board above my bed, and sometimes, like when I'm struggling to fall asleep or I'm talking on the phone, I'm looking at my vision board without thinking about it. That subliminal messaging to my brain does wonders!

A vision board can also help you make tough decisions. If you're having a hard time making a decision about something—you have two choices and both are tempting—refer to the goals on your board and evaluate which of the two options align better with your vision. Often you will find that a tempting choice does not do anything to help you achieve your goals—it only divides your attention. Giving your vision board a glance can help you keep your eyes on the prize without being distracted by shiny objects. We're all squirrels sometimes. Not to mention that—Wait, is that tinfoil? BRB.

If creating just one vision board will help you to become more self-aware, imagine how much you'll learn about yourself with your second vision board! You can literally track how you've grown as a person when you compare your first and second boards. What are you changing? What has become more or less important to you? My first vision board had several images of money on it. I can't say that I truly fulfilled that goal before making my second vision board, but still . . . money was not on my second one. Somewhere between my first and second board, money became less important to me. Maybe I realized that it didn't make me as happy as the other things I had on my board, such as travel and content creation. LOOK AT HOW SELF-AWARE I AM. Now I can focus my attention on travel and content creation and not chase easy money.

Before you run off to create a vision board, let's talk about visualization. In my life, I've practiced both long-term and short-term visualization, depending on the situation. Both have served me well on my journey to becoming a Bawse.

Long-term visualization is when you imagine yourself in a scenario that you hope will become a reality one day. You're not quite sure when or how it'll happen; all you know is that you want it to happen. In other words, you imagine the experience of obtaining all the things on your vision board. You can do this simply by sitting in a chair, closing your eyes, and imagining yourself signing the sales agreement for a new house. Feel free to even mimic signing your signature with your hand (bonus points if you hold a pen). Now, by *The Secret*'s logic, that's all you'd have to do to obtain a new house. But I don't believe that. The universe might respect the law of attraction, but it respects a good hustle even more. After you're done visualizing, get up and get to work.

You can also visualize with your eyes open by acting out something you want to happen and pretending it's real. Here's my favorite example. I used to desperately want to be interviewed on the radio. I would constantly hear celebrities doing plugs for radio stations while I was driving, like, "Hey, this is Usher and you're listening to Kiss 92.5." Every time I heard one of those plugs I would think, "Man that's so cool, and they're so famous!" So I started to imitate them. While driving in my car, I would pretend I was on the radio and I'd say a plug out loud to myself. I must have said, "Hey, this is your girl Superwoman and you're listening to Kiss 92.5, so keep it locked!" at least twenty-five times to myself before I ever got my first opportunity to do it on the radio in real life. The first time a radio host ever asked me to record a plug, I had to contain all my excitement and I was beyond prepared. Until then, I hadn't known how or when I would get there; I just knew I wanted to be on the radio.

Short-term visualization is helpful when you know you are going to be doing something specific and you want to imagine how the scenario will play out. For example, before a performance, I'll visualize exactly what I want to happen. I close my eyes, imagine myself walking onto the stage with full energy, and see the crowd's positive reaction. Then I watch myself perform in a way that makes me proud. I see how

" THE UNIVERSE MIGHT RESPECT THE LAW OF ATTRACTION, BUT IT RESPECTS A GOOD HUSTLE EVEN MORE.

I'm going to tell every joke, hit every bit of choreography, and nail my facial expressions. I'll even physically go through the motions with my eyes closed so that it feels as real as possible. It's like a dress rehearsal for the mind and spirit. When I open my eyes and do the show for real, the goal is to simulate what I visualized. There should be no issues since, according to my brain, this is round two.

We all know the cliché "See it, believe it, *achieve* it." We've probably taken a screenshot of it and shared it on Instagram thinking we were really deep. I definitely have (#MondayMotivation). Well, now you can actually give meaning to that quote by practicing the art of visualization. There is great power in knowing what you want and even greater power in pretending it's already yours. Combine that with a strong work ethic, and Christmas can come more than once a year.

Then you can start—Wait, is that a shiny ornament?! BRB.

CHAPTER 17

AIM HIGH

YOU SEE A CUSTOMER

eyeing a car at your dealership and you're unsure if they're going to buy it. You really want them to because you could use the commission and you have a quota to meet. The customer calls you over, acting mildly excited, but clearly trying to wear their best poker face. Let the games begin! You name a price. They begin to walk away. You lower the price. They suggest an even lower one. You start talking about the car's special features, and they pretend like they don't care that much. You say $50,000. The customer says $40,000. You say $49,000. They say $41,000. You make a final offer: $46,000.

"Fine! I'll pay $52,000." Said no buyer ever.

That's because when you negotiate, you're unlikely to get exactly what you asked for. And you definitely won't get MORE than what you asked for. I don't remember the last time I asked a friend to borrow their shirt and they replied, "Sure! And here's my cellphone and boyfriend too!" I mean, that would be a great friend, don't get me wrong, but it's just not that likely.

Life is one big negotiation. If I know one thing about bartering, it's that you need to start high. That's because you're never going to get exactly what you want, so you better ask for more than you need. When you go for something you want, there are three possible outcomes: ideal, workable, and horrible. A Bawse isn't scared to aim for ideal, because a Bawse knows that, at worst, they'll likely end up arriving at a workable scenario. But if you sell yourself short and play it safe, you may end up disappointed.

When my friend Humble and I were figuring out how to release our song "IVIVI" (Roman numerals for the area code for the city of Toronto, 416), we knew we wanted it to be epic. Humble had wanted to create a Toronto anthem for a long time, but we'd never gotten around to it because of our busy schedules. One day, as I was staring at the calendar, I noticed that the month of April was approaching. With a twinkle in my eye, I called Humble and told him we needed to release "IVIVI" on 4/16 and not a day later! I'm pretty sure I made that phone call on April 4 or so, in true last-minute Lilly fashion. This deadline forced us to write a song, record it, and plan a music video (see the chapter Set Deadlines) in less than two weeks.

Writing and recording the song was the easier part—with an assist from a few vodka-and-Sprites (to coat my vocal cords, obviously!). We finished the song in a few days and decided to spend the remaining four conceptualizing our music video. So there we were at my kitchen table, trying to think of a creative that could be pulled off in such a short amount of time. Shooting in a car, easy. Shooting downtown, easy. Shooting in a studio, easy. Then suddenly, with complete confidence and a straight face, I said, "You know what? We should shoot on the Raptors court inside the ACC." Humble just stared at me, expressionless. The Raptors are Toronto's NBA team and the ACC (Air Canada Centre) is the city's second-biggest stadium—the same stadium that promoters and artists pay thousands and thousands of dollars to use. And there I was, casually suggesting we should shoot our music video there—and in the next four days.

Humble chuckled and didn't say much, but I could read his mind. It would be next to impossible to get permission to shoot on that court, especially with such short notice and without a hefty check. I didn't want to give up so quickly, and so I made it my personal mission to at least TRY to make it happen. I contacted every person I knew—ticket sellers, social media strategists, even YouTube. (YouTube is like my third parent. If I don't know how to do something, I bug them and hope they can hold my hand and teach me.)

It turned out that YouTube has a relationship with the NBA, and my contact was able to connect me with someone from the Raptors team. Do you hear that? It's the sound of my determined foot slowly prying open a door. I put in my request: We wanted to shoot our music video on the Raptors court. We needed four hours. (I knew two would be

66 DON'T GIVE UP BEFORE YOU EVEN TRY.

more than enough.) We would have fifteen people with us (really, we only needed ten). We were going to use a drone (this part was true). The paperwork was submitted, and then the waiting game began. The response was that we would have to purchase various types of insurance to shoot inside the stadium—everything from insurance for ourselves to insurance for the drone. Well, ACC, I see your hand and I counter with "I think we only need this one insurance." Back and forth we went. Slowly I was able to get my foot in the door, until finally, two days later, we'd gotten the approval and were standing outside the ACC. We walked into the arena, set up our equipment at lightning speed, and shot the video in two hours, with ten people, using one drone.

A Bawse does not let anything stop them from aiming high. I ask crazy things of my team all the time and I won't accept anyone telling me something is "unrealistic." Don't give up before you even try. I refuse to believe something can't happen until I'm flat-out told NO. To be honest, sometimes even after hearing NO I still don't believe it can't be done. Why? Because I'm relentlessly determined. And you know what? It's worked out great for me so far. It's fine to push for what you want, as long as you're charming and polite about it.

If you aim low, you'll end up lower than you intended. That's why you have to aim high. No one else is going to compensate for your lack of ambition. I had the opportunity to shoot a collaboration video with First Lady Michelle Obama about the importance of education around the world. We both lead campaigns promoting education, and so doing a video together made perfect sense. When I confirmed the shoot, I was told I would have fifteen minutes with her. I asked for thirty. I got twenty. I wanted to play a game with her that lasted three rounds, and so I asked for five. I got three. I wanted to become the next president of the United States, and I said so. Everyone laughed. Apparently Canadians can't do that. Whatever. The point is, don't be afraid to ask for things. The worst that will happen is that you'll be told no. Just remember to smile, stand tall, and look as adorable as possible.

Now, I'd like you to give this book ten stars online. Ten complete stars, please.

What's that? You think it deserves only seven? Fine. What about eight?

You know what? Let's agree on five. Five stars will do.

Thanks!

smiles charmingly

CHAPTER 18

THE
ALPHABET
IS A
LIE

IF YOU'RE A PARENT,

you're likely going to hate this chapter. The next few pages go against a lot of the lessons I was taught while growing up, especially those that were drilled into me by my mom and dad. A lot of parents, especially South Asian parents (I say this from experience), are firm believers in having several backup plans when it comes to life. With respect to your career, finances, and even relationships (welp!), they stress how important it is to have a Plan A, Plan B, and Plan C. Hell, some parents even make it to a Plan E. Yes, that's right. A *plane* (Ba-Doom-Tish! I'm here all night, folks!).

The idea of a backup plan is ingrained in our minds. If I'm traveling for an event, I pack the outfit I'm going to wear complete with jewelry and shoes. Done. But then, what if for some unforeseen reason that outfit doesn't make sense anymore once I arrive? What if I spontaneously gain fifteen pounds on the plane ride because of turbulence or something? I better pack a backup outfit with another pair of shoes and some different jewelry. But then, neither of my outfits accounts for the weather being terrible. What if this one time Miami experiences a blizzard? I better pack a third outfit option that can withstand cold temperatures. Okay, done . . .

. . . although I never took into account the possibility of meeting some-one cute and being asked on a date. I better pack one nice outfit (and a razor) just to be safe. By the time I leave, I have my clothes in a U-Haul and I'm headed to the airport.

Backup plans for days! It's ironic that I'm constantly creating backups but still have yet to set up iCloud (I just don't get it, okay!). Oh well, that's not the point. The point is that regardless of how conditioned we are to create backup plans, I'm going to encourage you to focus only on Plan A. In other words, eff a Plan B.

When I made the decision to pursue YouTube full-time, I was in the middle of applying for graduate school. My parents were very keen on me getting my master's degree because they believed it would be something great to fall back on (you know, like a backup plan). So there I was, writing an essay for my application form, attempting to get into the counseling psychology program. Halfway through the essay I stopped and stared at the screen. I literally felt like I was Harry Potter and Dementors were eating away at my soul. And not even normal Dementors. They were Dementors that were on a no-carb diet or a juice cleanse or something and today was their cheat day. Basically, Dementors from Los Angeles.

I couldn't even get myself to finish the essay because this area of study just didn't excite me. The thought of getting into the program terrified me because I couldn't imagine going to school for two more years of my life. At that moment I slowly got out of my chair, walked to my parents' room (yes, I lived with my parents even during university; I said they were South Asian, remember? I didn't have a choice!), and announced that I didn't want to apply for graduate school, but instead wanted to pursue my YouTube career.

As you can imagine, this was a terrifying conversation for all of us. I was telling my parents that I didn't want to go to school and obtain a master's degree, but instead wanted to create videos for the Internet—something they didn't even know how to use. For my part, I was excited about my choice but also extremely scared. At the time I had only a few videos online and had no idea if my decision was at all realistic. In those days YouTube wasn't the known platform it is now. Today digital creators are business owners who have countless opportunities and revenue streams. We are getting recognized as tastemakers and influencers with real and powerful followings. But back in 2010, creating content for YouTube was a strange and unique phenomenon, especially in Toronto. The biggest creators had 2 or 3 million subscribers. Today people have over 40 million subscribers, and a video of a cat falling will get 3 million views. But in 2010, it was still unclear whether YouTube itself would stand the test of time. Who was to say that YouTube wouldn't go the way of MySpace and disappear?

My parents responded in the best way they possibly could: they gave me a year to try out YouTube full-time. If after a year I hadn't made any progress, they wanted me to pursue my master's. With that, I began my 365-day countdown and YouTube become my main focus.

Every day I wrote scripts, recorded videos, edited, watched other creators' videos, and researched marketing ideas. But I lived with a constant feeling of doubt, and a voice in the back of my head kept whispering: "But what if this doesn't work? You should still prepare for graduate school."

This carried on for a while until I received a sign from the universe. I was in Montreal for a small hosting gig and things were running late, so my friends and I were watching TV in our hotel room. Everyone was chatting away, drinking and doing their own thing, but I was fixated on the television. An interview with Kate Winslet was airing, and the host asked her, "What advice do you have for anyone that wants to act or get into the entertainment industry?" At that moment, it felt as if time slowed down, the entire room went quiet, and no one else was there except for Kate and me. Her answer was, essentially, "If you really want to do something, don't have a Plan B. Having a Plan B means you're expecting your Plan A to fail, and that isn't the right attitude." After her last word, I snapped back to reality with new clarity and purpose. I would toss my Plan B in the trash and put all my energy and efforts into my Plan A.

I started treating my career as if it was a guarantee. Instead of having a Plan B (graduate school) and Plan C (an office job), I developed a Plan A, Plan A 2.0, and Plan A 3.0. YouTube and entertainment were always going to be Plan A; the only things I would alter were my strategy and technique. When I was hit with obstacles such as low viewership, negative comments, or writer's block, I didn't give up and start considering other career paths. Instead I strengthened my Plan A by learning new ways to market myself, training my mind to deal with hate comments, and creating a creative space to write in.

Of course what I'm suggesting is risky, not to mention terrifying, but if you're willing to work for your dream, lose sleep for it, and give 200 percent for it, then put all your eggs in one basket and make the basket golden.

So what do you want to do? Who do you want to become? Where do you want to work? Whatever your answer is, make that your Plan A and don't clutter your mind with three other plans that are backups. Your mind, energy, and time need to be united for your Plan A to work.

I'll end by saying that I'm going to expect from you what all Indian parents expect from their children, and that's no B's, only A's. Get to work!

CHAPTER 19

IF YOU CAN
DO IT,
YOU DON'T HAVE TO
SAY IT

IF YOU TWEET

about going to hot yoga every day but no one is around to read it, will you still sweat?

Social media has gotten us into the habit of saying things instead of simply doing things. It's even led us to believe that saying something is the SAME as doing something. Of course, it's easy to convince people that what you say online is actually what you do offline. How would they know any better? You're behind a screen. Maybe you're actually at hot yoga, or maybe you're just in your apartment with the AC turned off and your legs mildly stretched out. But a Bawse knows that if you can do something, there's no need to say it.

Once upon a time, ever so long ago, I went on a date with a very handsome guy. I'm using "handsome" as a descriptor not because I'm superficial (although let's be real, it's a nice touch) but because I didn't know too much about him prior to this date. We met at a party and talked for a bit, but we were also drinking dranks (translation for old people: alcoholic beverages) and so we didn't really learn any deep information about each other. We just had the kind of stupid conversation you have while sipping a drink. Or two. Or seven. Whatever. No one was driving. (#BlessUpUberX)

I was excited to learn all about my handsome date and, admittedly, a little nervous. We ordered some drinks and sat across from each other, and I put all my energy into not blushing at the sight of his magnificent face. I asked him about his day and then he asked me about mine—you know, typical conversation. And then I asked him about work and he told me all about his career. And his goals. And his gym routine. And the most recent contract he'd signed. And what he was working on next. I sat in silence, listening to him. He told me stories all about how funny he was and how he makes everyone laugh at work. Then, without me asking, he told me all about how he was a really nice guy. In fact, he ended the story with, "And that's just the type of person I am." I knew I wasn't having THE BEST time, but I couldn't pinpoint why. I realized he wasn't asking me very many questions, but I chalked that up to nerves. You know, trying to give people the benefit of the doubt. But even when he did ask me a question here or there, I still was having a 7/10 time on a date that I was expecting to be a 20/10 (okay, fine, that was superficial of me).

When I got home, my friend asked me how it went. I said, "Honestly, I don't know." I had to sit down, take time out of my day, bust out a calculator, open an encyclopedia, and start an intensive research process to determine what it was I hadn't liked about the date. Then I figured it out. He'd kept TELLING me about the type of person he was, but he'd done nothing to SHOW me.

If you're funny, you shouldn't have to notify people that you're funny. And not to be a jerk, but I didn't laugh once on that date. Yet he told me two different stories about how funny his friends thought he was. If you're nice, you don't have to tell people you're nice; they'll be able to see that.

If you're going to talk the talk, then you have to walk the walk. In fact, if you can walk the walk, I really see no need for you to do any talking unless you're specifically asked about the walk you are providing. LESS TALKING. MORE WALKING.

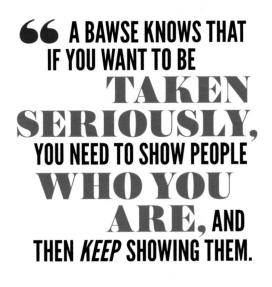

People often say "words lie and actions speak the truth." I used to think that was a great saying, but then I heard a motivational speaker by the name of Trent Shelton say something even better. He said, "Words lie; actions can lie too. Consistency speaks the truth." My jaw dropped at the accuracy of these words. Talking about something doesn't make it true. And action is only meaningful if it's consistent. A Bawse knows that if you want to be taken seriously, you need to show people who you are, and then *keep* showing them.

Don't tell your boss you work hard; let your work prove it. Don't just tell your girlfriend you're loyal; *be* loyal. Don't tell your opponent you're going to knock them out; just knock them out.

Talk is cheap, so leave it at the thrift store.

CHAPTER 20

KNOW
THE
GAME

YOU KNOW WHAT THEY SAY:

"You have to play the game to change the game." But how do you play the game if you don't know the game? You can't. You'd be dribbling a basketball on a tennis court and yelling for a penalty. And if you can't change the game because you can't play the game because you don't know the game . . . you're definitely not going to win the game. Right now you might be thinking, "WHAT GAME?! I'm an accountant!" Well, my fellow Bawse, the reality is that almost everything in life is a game. And "game" isn't a synonym for something unimportant, nor does it have to give you that icky feeling. Games are great. Most things in life involve strategy, rules, levels, and players. When you're at a bar and hit on a cute girl, that's using strategy in the dating game. When you set yourself apart as an overachieving assistant and get promoted, you passed a level in the office game. When you agree to play hide-and-seek with your baby sister to get out of trouble with your mother, you're playing the game as well. In fact, you're playing two games.

Whatever you're doing in life, whether you're a doctor, painter, student, or lemonade stand owner, it's important to know the game so that you can excel at playing it. One of the best ways to do this is to become aware of what everyone else in the same field is doing. Not only does this give you the ability to learn from other people's successes and mistakes, but it also encourages healthy competition, which is necessary for evolution. In addition, knowing the other players in the game can help you adjust your strategy accordingly, just like a coach who studies the formations and plays of an opposing team.

Before I went on my first tour, I made it a priority to attend as many shows by fellow digital creators as I could. Of course I went because I wanted to support my friends, but I also wanted to gain as much knowledge and insight from the experience as possible. Instead of trying to blindly write a creative for my own show, I wanted to see what everyone else was offering first. I took notes on what I loved, what I thought could be improved, how the crowd was reacting, and how long the show was. Was there a dedicated stage manager? How many seats were VIP? Where was security positioned? Were there costume changes? How many? How often? I absorbed all the information around me and used it to develop my own strategy. I wanted to make sure that whatever I offered was not only up to par but different from what was already out there. If you're trying to set yourself apart, you need to know what has already been done.

I also watch YouTube videos when I'm taking a break from work. Yes, when I take a break from making a YouTube video, I watch a YouTube video (#ReasonsImSingle). The reason I do this is

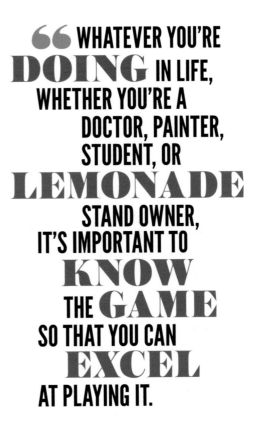

WHATEVER YOU'RE DOING IN LIFE, WHETHER YOU'RE A DOCTOR, PAINTER, STUDENT, OR LEMONADE STAND OWNER, IT'S IMPORTANT TO KNOW THE GAME SO THAT YOU CAN EXCEL AT PLAYING IT.

because I think it's important to be familiar with the content that exists alongside mine. If I'm working on a video called "I Like Potatoes" and then I go online and see four other videos called "I Like Potatoes," well, that's not great. That is above the recommended daily carbohydrate intake for any viewer. Similarly, I don't want to be creating content on my webcam, with mediocre lighting and basic transition, if everyone else on the trending page is using an SLR, ring light, and complicated animations. I want to stay in the league, so I keep up to date on the game.

Knowing the game not only helps you play to the best of your ability but also prevents you from being cheated. Imagine playing a game of poker and not really knowing the rules. You have three sixes and two kings and your opponent has a pair of fours. After you reveal your cards uncertainly, your opponent notices and confidently claims victory, therefore taking all your chips. You had a full house and didn't know it! You're like the Olsen twins before they were old enough to form memories. Cut. It. Out.

Whenever I have to review a contract, I take my time with it. Admittedly, the legal world isn't a game I know completely, and that's why, when I'm forced to play, I consult with other players. The best part about the game of life is that we're on so many teams at the same time. There have been many times when I've received a contract and something has seemed off, so I call up my creator friends and ask about their thoughts and experiences. At a different time I might be playing against these creators in a different game, but in the legal game they're my allies. In more than one instance I've discovered that I'd been given incorrect information, or to be blunt, I'd been lied to. But again, it's all a game. The people doing business with me are playing their game, and as a result, I have to play mine. And I will.

Recognizing that you're playing a game doesn't just make things more fun (who doesn't love games?) but also helps you understand why people do the things they do, allowing you to react with rationality, not emotion. An agent who sends me a contract that is heavily in their favor isn't necessarily trying to hurt my feelings; they're playing the game. That understanding allows me to respond with my own strategic move, instead of with emotion. When a basketball player crosses you over, they aren't trying to break your heart; they're trying to get points to win the game. Similarly, if you're the person who gets crossed over, it's in your best interest to get better, not bitter. Getting better helps your game; getting bitter does not.

Whatever game you're in, strap on some knee pads and get ready to play—unless your game doesn't impact your knees at all, in which case you'd just look silly. Us fellow Bawses will be cheering you on.

Let's play.

66

I WANT TO STAY IN THE LEAGUE, SO I KEEP UP TO DATE ON THE GAME.

99

CHAPTER 21

CLIMB
THE
LADDER

UNLESS YOU'RE BORN

into a royal family, chances are you will have to start from the bottom and work your way up in life. If that sentence doesn't apply to you, then HI, PRINCE HARRY! Thanks for buying my book—or, you know, demanding it. Whatever.

If you want to be the CEO of a company, you might have to start out as a sales rep. If you want to be a director, you may have to get your foot in the door by being a production assistant. If you want to be an actor, you will likely have to fight your way into auditions. Many situations in life require us to climb an invisible ladder, and it's not usually an easy climb. You have to earn each rung.

When I first started out on YouTube, I was thirsty for knowledge and wisdom. I lived in Toronto, but most of my peers were living in L.A. and were inaccessible to me. I was yearning to make meaningful connections with other creators, and so when I discovered that Harley Morenstein from Epic Meal Time, a very big YouTube channel, was in my city, I instantly tweeted him. Truth be told, I wasn't expecting a reply. At the time I had around 100,000 subscribers and Harley's following was a lot bigger than mine. But to my surprise, Harley messaged me back and said he'd love to sit down together. He had a meeting but would message me after. He was staying in a hotel downtown, about thirty minutes from my house. I was overjoyed that he responded, and from that point on I was glued to my phone. Every four minutes I would check my direct messages to ensure I didn't miss anything. Then it occurred to me that Harley had never actually told me what time his meeting was and so I had no idea when we would meet. What if he finished his meeting and then had only fifteen minutes to spare and I was thirty minutes away? Or even worse, what if he messaged during rush hour and it took me an hour and a half to get downtown? Those were risks I simply could not take. I texted two of my friends and told them we were going downtown for no reason at all. Like good friends (who also had no choice), they agreed.

I spent the entire evening roaming around downtown to ensure I was in close proximity to Harley if he messaged me. As it got later, our roaming was reduced to just sitting in a car parked on the side of the street somewhere downtown. What if he didn't message? Or what if he messaged saying he could no longer make time? These questions were valid, but I continued to sit in the car with my friends, some good music, and a whole lot of faith. Soon enough my phone pinged, and to my relief it was Harley saying he had just finished his meetings and was free to meet. Well, would you look at that—I was already downtown! WHAT A COINCIDENCE!

My two friends and I met Harley and I had a great forty-five-minute conversation with him. He taught me so much about YouTube and brand deals and gave me advice that helped shape the career I have today. The guidance I got from Harley that evening gave me the boost I needed to move up from the first rung of the ladder I was on. You could even say that he reached down from several rungs above and gave me a helping hand.

I hope that story was motivating, but I realize it might also sound a little stalkerish, which I'm okay with. Harley and I are friends now and I'm confident he would be okay with me stalking him anytime.

This wasn't the only time I did something ridiculous in hopes of establishing a meaningful connection with someone I find inspirational. A few years ago I was sitting at the airport waiting to board a flight. As soon as they called my zone number, I heard my phone ping. It was a direct message on Twitter. I opened it and instantly lost all chill. The friend I was traveling with thought I was having heart failure because I froze with my jaw dropped. The message was from MIA (only one of the best female rappers ever!) and said, "Hey, can we do something?" Casually. MIA. Messaging me. To do something. Extremely frazzled, I got on the plane and responded as quickly as possible before being forced to go into airplane mode. I came up with "I'd love to! Tell me where and when." I'M SO ORIGINAL AND FUNNY AND SOCIAL.

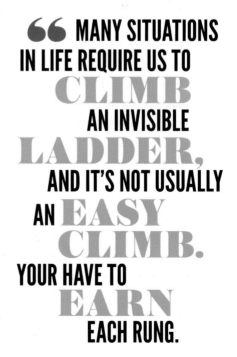

66 MANY SITUATIONS IN LIFE REQUIRE US TO CLIMB AN INVISIBLE LADDER, AND IT'S NOT USUALLY AN EASY CLIMB. YOUR HAVE TO EARN EACH RUNG.

For the entire plane ride I was anxious because I had no idea what her reply would be. What if her account had been hacked? What if it was her son? What if she'd gotten mixed up and thought I was someone else? People tell me I look like Bruno Mars all the time! When the plane landed, before I did anything else I checked my messages, and squealed when I saw her reply: "Tell me when you're in NYC." Well, as fate would have it, I had a gig in NYC the very next week. I'm not being a stalker and making that up—I did actually have a gig. Perfect! I responded and we agreed to meet up in a few days.

I am a fan of MIA's work and really admire what she does, so I didn't want to arrive empty-handed. Over the next week I arranged for one of my friends to create a custom art piece that I could gift her. The turnaround time was so rushed that I got the piece delivered to the airport before I left for NYC. When I landed in New York, the experience was very similar to my initial meeting with Harley: I knew which day MIA wanted to meet, but I had no other information and was banking on a reply.

The day we were supposed to meet, I was leaving my hotel room early in the morning to attend some meetings and knew I wouldn't be back until later that night. I hadn't heard from MIA in the last few days and the whole meeting seemed to be unlikely. Discouraged, I looked at the painting as I exited my room. *Well, that was a waste.* Then a tiny voice inside my head said, "What if she replies?" That was enough for me to turn around and pick up the painting. It was too large to fit in a bag, so I committed to carrying it under my arm around the city for the entire day, just in case she messaged back. Hours passed and I was still carrying this annoying thing around. People were staring at me, my friend was making fun of me, and I was beating myself up. I stopped at a curb to sit down and take a break. As a last-ditch effort, I pulled out my phone and messaged MIA, asking what time and where she'd like to meet. Seconds later she replied and gave me the address of an ice cream shop in Brooklyn. Within the hour I was eating ice cream with MIA and her son, gift in hand, smile on my face. During our conversation, she taught me so much about the music industry and gave me legal advice I'd never heard before. That experience helped me climb yet another rung on the ladder.

These encounters may seem like minor ridiculous things, and you might even think that I was devaluing myself by waiting around for people, but the conversations I had were essential and motivated me to continue my work. When you're climbing the ladder, the heaviest piece of clothing you wear is often your pride. In my opinion, waiting hours to meet these two people doesn't mean I don't know my worth; it means I think they're worth my time. Both Harley and MIA knew more than I did and had knowledge they were willing to share with me.

The thing about the ladder is that no matter how high a rung you reach, there will always be people above you. And sometimes the people above you will throw stones at you to try to knock you down. This behavior can be intentional or unintentional. Sometimes they might not even realize their feet are kicking dust onto you. The people above you on the ladder aren't necessarily rich, famous jerks who look down on everyone else. It's not about status. That's the wrong attitude to have. I believe that the people above me on the ladder have more experience and expertise than I do, and I can accept and respect that.

Even today, regardless of the fact that I've established myself as a content creator with a large following, I get stones thrown at me from the rungs above. I've done countless collaborations with movie stars and musicians, but when a new one is presented to me, I still have to go to hell and back to make it happen. I'm required to send three script ideas, and when the producers don't like any of those, I'm asked to send three more by the next morning as if that's an easy thing to do. Once I get a script approved I'm told I have fifteen minutes to shoot a video that will probably take sixty minutes. The video can only be shot on a day when I'm already completely booked, so now I have to rearrange my schedule. What do I do? I could reply with a middle-finger emoji, but that wouldn't be very productive. I put my pride aside and smile throughout the process, as long as the outcome results in an awesome video I'm proud of. That's climbing the ladder. No one said that some rungs wouldn't be covered in BS.

It's a hard ladder to climb. There will be obstacles, exhaustion, and sometimes even a few snakes along the way (now it's the Snakes and Ladders game). But when you climb the ladder you learn lessons, build character, and earn knowledge. The worst thing you can do is act entitled when you are at the bottom of the ladder, refusing to get sweaty. It doesn't work like that.

Sometimes to be inspired, successful, or supported you need to sit in a car on the side of the road for three hours. Other times you might have to be that crazy lady carrying a huge painting. Maybe it'll be worth it or maybe it won't be. Either way, you keep climbing like a Bawse.

CHAPTER 22

TAKE THE STAIRS

<------------------->

WE'RE ALWAYS TRYING

to look for shortcuts. It's in our nature. I don't have to unlock my phone to take a picture because I can just swipe up. When my GPS can save me sixty seconds on the road, it'll reroute me. Worst-case scenario, if I do have to unlock my phone (annoying!), then I can just scan my finger because who has time to input four numbers? I don't even have to type a full sentence when TXTING b/c abbreviations are v easy 2 understand FYI and acceptable AF BTW. Who has time to meet new people and establish meaningful relationships? Instead I can just swipe left or right on your image and let superficial computing do the work. Shortcuts save us time and energy; let's face it, they're convenient. However, a Bawse knows that shortcuts do not exist when it comes to success.

People often ask me what my secret to success is, and I think they expect me to give them some sort of spell to cast. It would make them feel at ease if I told them how wizardry and a drop of lion's blood got me where I am. That way they could stop having to work hard and instead focus on getting a lion. Unfortunately, that isn't the case, so leave Simba alone (hasn't he been through enough?!). My secret to success is exactly what most people don't want to hear: it's a ton of hard work.

There is no escalator to success. You have to take the stairs. (I know, I know, the last chapter was about a ladder, but hear me out.) I am not the product of a viral video. I didn't have a massive hit that got me a ton of subscribers and views that I based my career on (not that anything is wrong with that). Instead, over the course of my career, every single video has given me recognition and subscribers. If I ask fans how they discovered me, their answers will all be different. With each video I put out, I take a step upward on the staircase to success, leaving a strong foundation of content below me. I don't care if it's a small or big step, as long as the movement is upward.

Having said that, an escalator definitely does exist, especially in my industry. Creating content that puts other people down, using clickbait thumbnails, and promoting misleading video titles are all ways people choose to take an escalator. You'll likely get a lot of views and become really popular, but for how long? Your foundation isn't solid because it was built too quickly or dishonestly. Would you rather travel on a bridge constructed over the course of a year or one that was thrown together in forty-eight hours? An escalator can go out of service at any time, but the stairs are always there. How many times have you heard a hit song from someone and then never heard of them again? How many times have you seen a viral video of someone doing something absolutely disgusting and then never seen their face again? Escalators exist in every industry, but a Bawse will always take the stairs and prioritize the longevity of their career. Gimmicks and shortcuts aren't the best materials to build with. All it takes is one strong wind to knock it all down.

It's absolutely exhausting to climb the stairs, especially because you can't always see the top of the staircase. It just seems like a never-ending ascent. As a result, even when people are told that stairs are THE ONLY WAY TO SUCCESS, they will still try to create a shortcut. *What if I hire Optimus Prime to carry me up the stairs? What if I buy the staircase? What if I tell people that receiving piggybacks is part of my religion? Or what if this map is inaccurate to begin with and there's a faster path through the mountains?*

Hear me when I say you MUST start climbing and do the work. No ifs, ands, or buts. Remember all those times you had a major project to finish and you just stared at it, thinking, "What if I get a doctor's note?" All right, great, you faked a stomachache and got a note. Now what? You still have to do the assignment. Then you think, "Maybe I'll just copy off a friend." Your teacher caught you and now you have to do the assignment again. No matter how many times you stare at this project, it's not going anywhere. Why? Because you just need to buckle down and do the work. There is no other way, so stop wasting time convincing yourself there is.

I know that deep down inside you know this. It's just like how I know that Googling "how to get nice abs without working out" is never going to be productive. The answer is to eat right and work out. No matter how many juices I drink or electronic devices I strap to my stomach, I will not get nice abs. Similarly, no matter how many gimmicks or shortcuts you try, you won't succeed unless you do the work.

"

A BAWSE KNOWS THAT SHORTCUTS DO NOT EXIST WHEN IT COMES TO SUCCESS.

"

It's important to note that there is a huge difference between taking the stairs and being inefficient. While climbing the stairs, I do many things that save me time. Let me give you an example:

TASK: I have an amazing video idea that is going to require a lot of work.

TAKING AN ESCALATOR: I'll just do an easier video and make it look cool in the thumbnail.

TAKING THE STAIRS WITH EFFICIENCY: Let me put time and effort into assembling a team that will help me execute this great idea. That way I can focus on being in the video while all the paperwork and other details are handled by someone else.

You might be yelling right now, saying, "WELL, LILLY, not everyone has an assistant and a team to help them!" Yeah, well, I didn't have an assistant or team at the bottom of the staircase either. I was only able to hire a team after climbing the stairs solo for years.

Working hard feels good. Of course it's exhausting and stressful and causes you to miss a party or two, but at the end of the day it is so rewarding. One of the best feelings in the world is when you know that luck didn't play a role in your success. Doing work eliminates the need for luck. I'm not lucky, I just took the stairs. And you should too.

I told you this wasn't going to be a fairy tale. There is no magic carpet or genie. There's just you and a staircase, so start stretching and take the first step.

With everything else, feel free to use shortcuts. K, G2G, plz keep reading for more LOLs, ILY.

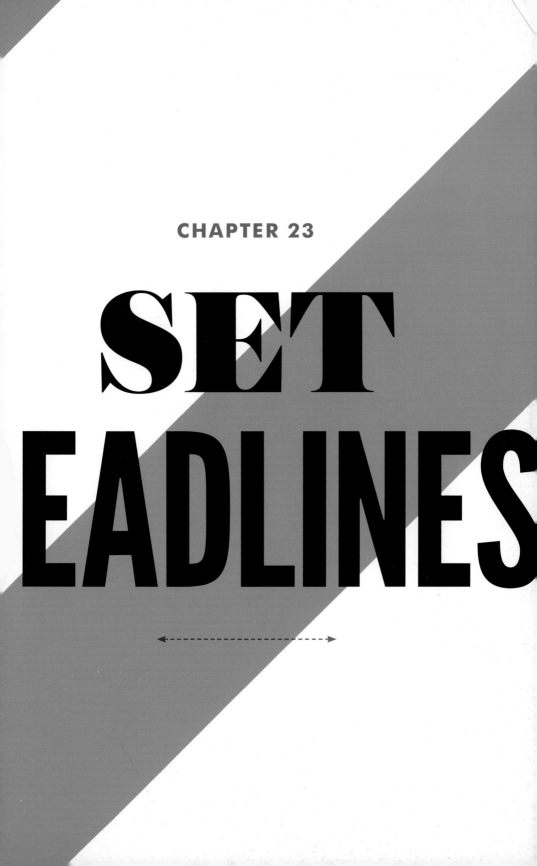

CHAPTER 23

SET
EADLINES

REMEMBER THAT SCENE

from *300* where Leonidas is getting pierced with arrows from every direction, but he continues attacking his enemy until his last breath? It's stressful and painful to watch as he swings his sword with aggression and purpose. Deep down you know that it's the end, but his persistence gives you a little shred of hope. That's what I looked like in high school the night before a major project was due. I had three weeks to get this twenty-page essay done, but lo and behold there I was at eleven o'clock on a Sunday night guzzling down my third can of Coke. I'd tried to write the essay the previous Sunday, but I couldn't find a comfortable enough pen to create an outline, so I had to go supply shopping. A few days later I'd tried again, but it turned out my desk was too messy to work on, so I had to clean my room. And the basement. And mow the lawn. And, for the first time in my life, do my laundry. The day before, I had been committed to doing this essay but I sneezed a few times and decided to take it easy and watch some medicinal TV instead.

Procrastination is a hustler's worst enemy. It's that little voice inside of us that craves instant gratification and convinces us that almost anything can be put off for later, no matter how unrealistic. As a result, you will wait until the last possible minute to start your assignment, leave your house for a meeting, or change your car's oil. In most cases you'll get the task done somehow, some way. Maybe it wasn't done to the best of your ability, but you probably still got it done. Now, imagine how powerful procrastination would be if you had absolutely no deadline at all—completing the work was merely good for you. You would be seventy-two years old and in an old folks' home trying to finish your math homework from the tenth grade. And even then you would convince yourself that your wheelchair wasn't comfortable enough, so you'd get to that homework later.

Throughout most of my life, deadlines were put in place for me because someone else was in charge: a professor, my parents, or my boss. When I decided to take control of my own life and become an entrepreneur, no one was around to tell me what to do and when to do it. With that reality came a beautiful freedom. And with that freedom came the possibility of making bad choices. If it was a random Monday and I wanted to sleep the entire day, no one was going to stop me. I quickly learned that I had to be my own boss and set deadlines for myself, or I would go nowhere fast. I created a schedule that required me to upload a video on my channel every Monday and Thursday. The CEO of YouTube isn't ever going to write me up if I don't deliver—the only person I have to answer to is me. This upload schedule prevents me from overthinking and procrastinating and prompts me to get things done. It's a major reason for my success.

As you can imagine, creating deadlines takes a huge amount of self-control, and that's why sometimes you have to force them upon yourself. For years I would tell myself that "one day" I'd move to Los Angeles. The comfort of home and the tediousness of obtaining legal documentation caused me to put off the move. One month I blamed the delay on a family vacation; another month I was sick; the month after that was my birthday and, well, it takes me thirty days to plan a party. Finally, during one business trip to L.A., I decided to take a step forward and go apartment hunting. I scoped out about five or six places and conveniently disliked them. Yet again I had to delay my plan. At this point, setting a deadline in my mind wasn't enough to make things happen. I needed to force myself to make the move, so I sent an email out to my team that said on December 1 I would be moving to L.A. That was in four months. I called my insurance company and told them to cancel my car insurance effective December 1. I did the same with my cellphone provider. I created a situation in which I wouldn't be able to function in Toronto on December 2, thus forcing me to move before that date.

One month prior to moving I still didn't have an apartment in L.A. I told myself that no matter what, on December 1, I would move. If that meant staying at a hotel with all my boxes, then so be it. That would be my own fault. Two weeks prior to moving I had some business in Los Angeles, so I made one last attempt to find an apartment. One, two, three down and no luck. Hotel it is! However, the very last apartment I looked at, two weeks before moving, hours before heading back to Toronto, was perfect. It was a little more expensive than I was hoping for, but my deadline didn't allow me to overthink. Within twenty-four hours I signed the lease. A few days later I ordered furniture. A few days after that I had a going-away party. That night I packed all my stuff, and the next morning I moved to Los Angeles.

This is an extreme example of deadline setting, and I'd be lying if I said it wasn't absolutely terrifying to not have an apartment two weeks prior to moving. However, the lesson I learned is one that has helped me throughout my career: force deadlines. Sometimes I find myself sitting on a video idea for way too long. I'll come up with a great concept that cannot be executed in one day, and so I'll hold on to it with the hope that I'll have more free time later. I won't. I never do. Instead, I now confirm a shoot date and hire an entire crew even before I have a script or confirmed actors. Writing a date on my calendar and setting a deadline forces me to find the time to get my act together. When I want to collaborate with other creators, I do the same thing. I'll confirm a date for us to shoot and I'll have absolutely no idea what the creative is until the night before. It's stressful and sometimes a bit overwhelming, but I always get it done, every single time.

For larger projects or goals such as "open my own restaurant" or "write a movie script," it's harder to set just one deadline. Instead, it may be smarter to break the goal down into small pieces and assign each of those pieces a specific deadline. For example, instead of saying that you are going to "write a movie script," break your goal down into smaller, more manageable pieces, such as "create a log line," "finish character outline," "create mood board," etc. If you need to force yourself to stick to those deadlines, set meetings with partners or friends and commit to sharing your ideas with them on a certain date. Deadlines are always easier to follow when they're public and you're held accountable for them. This is why I publicly promote my video schedule. If Monday and Thursday uploads were my little secret, then my week would simply never have a Monday or Thursday. I would practice a five-day week. The moon would have to adjust accordingly.

Think of something you've been wanting to do for a long time but have never gotten around to. I want you to take a second and look deep inside yourself. Do you REALLY want to accomplish this task? Are you willing to work your absolute hardest for it? Are you willing to acknowledge that your hardest isn't your hardest, and then work even harder than that? If the answer is yes, grab a calendar and set a deadline.

Can't think of anything? Let me help you out. You will finish reading this book by _____.

The clock is ticking.

"

PROCRASTINATION
IS A HUSTLER'S
WORST ENEMY.

"

CHAPTER 24

DON'T BE MADE.

DON'T BE BROKEN.

←- - - - - - - - - - - - - - - →

YOU'RE TAKING A MAJOR TEST,

applying for a job, auditioning for a movie, starting a sales pitch, or making a presentation to your entire school. Whatever it is, you're about to do something important and you're thinking that if it doesn't work out, your life is literally over. You might as well be Kenny from *South Park* because there's no hope for you. You need this. Your entire existence depends on this! You are a mere mortal and this success is essential to your survival. It's basically oxygen!

To this I say: STOP. I don't want you to be gasping for air like a fish out of water when you have something important to do. If you think about it, it's quite terrifying and, to be blunt, stupid to base your entire education or career on one opportunity. Of course some things in life are very important, but a Bawse understands that no one thing should make or break you.

You are building an empire, and you should know that empires are not built overnight and they do not fall easily. They should be built on a strong foundation so that they withstand the test of time and are resilient when threatened. Empires are not built upon a single pillar and, similarly, your career should not be built on a single success. One success is a terrific building block, but it's not the only thing supporting you. If you land a promotion at work, your empire isn't resting on this one promotion. Your previous work experience, school degree, and great technical skills all act as pillars that hold you up. Similarly, one pillar crumbling away does not destroy an entire empire; therefore, one failure should not destroy everything you've built.

In other words, if one opportunity will make or break your success, then your idea of success isn't solid enough to begin with. Even if you get the job, ace the test, or kill the sales pitch, you can't bank your entire success on one achievement.

But I get it. When you're faced with a great opportunity, your mind can get a bit carried away and dramatic. Throughout my career I've received many opportunities to collaborate on videos with some pretty cool people, including Selena Gomez, Priyanka Chopra, Shay Mitchell, and Arnold Schwarzenegger. Every time I'm presented with one of these opportunities, I struggle to come up with a video idea, which is strange since I normally pump out two creative videos a week. But I end up convincing myself that no idea is good enough for this once-in-a-lifetime collaboration. After all, this collaboration is with someone epic and it needs to be better than anything else I've ever done! What if 1 million new people who've never heard of me watch this video? What if my entire future on

"YOU CAN'T BANK YOUR ENTIRE SUCCESS ON ONE ACHIEVEMENT. YOUR SUCCESS SHOULDN'T WALK ON STILTS.

YouTube depends on this one collaboration? I rack my brain trying to think of something spectacular, and if all goes well, I finally write a creative I feel confident about. I shoot the video, edit it, and upload it, expecting it to alter the trajectory of my entire career. I patiently sit in my office chair waiting for the president to call me and offer me some sort of award. Perhaps they'll let me walk on the moon. Better yet, someone will give me the key to the moon! Well, first they'll build a door on the moon and then they'll give me the key. Either way, I'm getting a key!

But then nothing happens. Sure, the video will garner some buzz and maybe even receive a few more views than usual. But after a day or two, things go back to normal. In fact, many of my solo videos have done better than some of my biggest collaborations. After waiting for the key to the moon several times, I've learned that a super-cool collaboration isn't ever going to be the thing that "makes" my career. Instead, my career is the sum of everything I do.

Other times I've made videos that weren't received well. While scrolling through the negative comments I'd think, "This is the end. My career is over." But it never is. Next week I post two more videos and the previous one is forgotten. I wouldn't have much of a YouTube channel if one bad video caused the entire thing to collapse. That's the position I want to be in, one that allows for mistakes and growth in equal measure.

I enter auditions with this same mentality. Of course I want to do my absolute best in an audition room, but before I enter I say to myself, "This

66

IF ONE OPPORTUNITY WILL MAKE OR BREAK YOUR SUCCESS, THEN YOUR IDEA OF SUCCESS ISN'T SOLID ENOUGH TO BEGIN WITH.

99

isn't going to make or break you." This puts my nerves at ease and allows me to stay calm. If I nail the audition and get the role, that's amazing, but my career still won't be defined by that one role. My empire is made up of my YouTube channel, my book, my collaborations, my social campaigns, and my partnerships.

Having said all this, I'm not suggesting you should approach important opportunities with nonchalance. You should always give 110 percent of your energy and effort. But at the same time you want to be in a position where you cannot be impacted so easily. You can be the ruler of a strong empire but still have the mentality of a hungry hustler.

So if you find yourself stressing over one opportunity or one failure, perhaps the real problem is the foundation you've built. A Bawse cannot walk the walk if the ground is crumbling beneath them. You need to strengthen your empire.

You are not a teetering tower. Your career is not standing on one leg getting a Breathalyzer test on the side of the road. Your success is not a game of Jenga. You cannot be made or broken so easily.

Build Your Empire

List all the pillars that make up your success and that will NOT allow you to be made or broken with ease.

1. _____

_____

2. _____

_____

3. _____

_____

4. _____

_____

CHAPTER 25

YOU'RE AN ARCHITECT

SOCIAL MEDIA

has made everyone insecure. Don't get me wrong—if I could, I would marry YouTube, and I'm completely in love with Twitter because it provides me with endless entertainment and information (and memes—lots and lots of wonderful, glorious memes). But social media also exposes us to what everyone else is doing. And let's be real: according to Facebook, everyone we know is happy, always dressed to impress, at the gym, politically correct, eating right, and constantly cuddling a cute puppy. When you're going through a rough patch and doubting your very existence, seeing Kelly from your social studies class on the beach with a martini and a hot boyfriend isn't very helpful. That's because we compare other people's highlight reels to our blooper reel and accept that illusion as reality.

We all do it. There have been so many times when I've had a day full of rejection and failure and then I sign on to Facebook only to see that two of my high school friends just got married. I'm sitting there, single, trying to make it in Hollywood, alone in my apartment, eating burnt popcorn for dinner, and just staring at this wedding reception album thinking, "What the hell am I doing with my life? Am I completely delusional? Should I be getting married? I don't even remember the last time I was in a relationship! I AM LITERALLY NOT DOING LIFE CORRECTLY."

Then a few weeks later I'll connect with one of my newly married friends and they will tell me how they got into a fight with their wife and then signed on to Facebook only to see a picture of me with Michelle Obama at the White House. They began to think, "What the hell am I doing in my life? Here I am getting married, spending time on floral arrangements instead of my career! What if I fail at my job? What if I never make it to the White House? I AM LITERALLY NOT DOING LIFE CORRECTLY."

Here's the thing, though. There is no correct way of living life. Similarly, there's no one path that leads to success. A Bawse knows that there are many different pathways to every destination in life, and just because

you've only been given one set of directions, that doesn't mean ten other roads don't all lead to the same place.

Throughout my life I believed that the only way to make it in Hollywood was to audition over and over again for movie roles. That's all I was ever exposed to in films and through stories people told me. You have to move to L.A., struggle a lot, have a side job, and audition many times until one day you finally land a role. After moving to L.A., I realized that auditioning over and over again was only one way to achieve success in Hollywood. My career on YouTube was actually paving a new pathway to the same end goal. You see, the audition process is very grueling and competitive. There can be ten people who are all great for a role and yet someone is chosen over the others for reasons no one will ever really understand. Looks, height, weight, accent, ethnicity—all of these characteristics can factor into the decision. My success on YouTube gives me something special, and that is a following. When I walk into an audition, the casting agent knows that I bring a very large online audience with me and that my audience is ready to support me in my future projects.

At first I was very skeptical about the entire thing. I didn't like the idea of getting opportunities because I had a following online. I should have to audition over and over again while juggling three jobs because that's what people said I had to do. I expressed my discontent to my good friend Humble, saying, "I don't want to be given opportunities because I have a following, I want to work for opportunities." His reply changed my entire perspective on the situation. He said: "You weren't born with your following. You worked for it."

He was absolutely correct. My following is the result of countless all-nighters, years of hard work, and an unwavering work ethic. Why shouldn't I create a new path to success in Hollywood via YouTube? Why shouldn't I change the game? Why shouldn't I create a new L.A. fairy tale?

Don't get me wrong. I still have to audition for things over and over again and practice my acting. My online following doesn't land me movie roles *that* easily. If that were the case, I'd be Katniss Everdeen, but I am not. (Though I could be. Just a note for any directors reading this who are considering a spin-off franchise: I'm proficient in whistling.) However, my success on YouTube does allow me to take a path less frequently walked. My loyal following has gotten me into meetings with Mindy Kaling and Whitney Cummings. Auditioning didn't get me into those rooms; my online presence did. Mindy discovered my videos online and she liked my work. That's what got me in to see her.

When people ask me for advice about the digital space, I always start by saying, "I can tell you about the route I took, but I'm not familiar with the entire map." I say that because I believe new paths can be created every single day. We live in an exciting time where almost anything is possible. All you need to do is use your unique mind to create a path that works for you. Think about it. Each pathway has only so much room. You don't want to be that awkward third wheel who's forced to walk on the grass because of a crowded path, do you? No, you don't. You're not Milhouse.

Think about where you want to get in life, what you want to achieve, and where you want to be years from now. Now think about the directions you've been given to get there. I want you to pretend like there is an earthquake and the roads between you and your goal are cracking. How are you going to get to your destination? Find two or three more paths that all lead to the same place. That's how you should view the road map to success. It's not a straight line, but a loopy, curvy maze that resembles one of those puzzles on the back of a cereal box.

You're standing in the middle of a blank piece of paper. Unleash your inner architect and design your path to success. Get wild, be creative, and don't get distracted by the flow of traffic.

Traffic sucks anyway.

"

YOU'RE STANDING IN THE MIDDLE OF A BLANK PIECE OF PAPER. UNLEASH YOUR INNER ARCHITECT AND DESIGN YOUR PATH TO SUCCESS.

"

CHAPTER 26

BE ACTIVE

I AM LITERALLY

LOLing as I write this chapter because I'm the least qualified person to do so. Ask me to pull an all-nighter and I will. Ask me to go on tour for two months and do two shows a day and I'll do it with a smile on my face. But ask me to do twenty sit-ups and I will run away from home, throw my phone into the ocean so no one can reach me, and hide in the deepest, darkest corner of the earth. Since I stopped dancing professionally years ago, I haven't been very good at keeping active. I tell myself it's because I have no time—I'm always busy working. But as I grow older and hustle harder, I'm learning that being active and keeping my body healthy is part of my job.

Being active has nothing to do with being sexy, sculpting a six-pack, or fitting into a smaller size. It's about making sure your body can keep up with your hustle. Having an amazing work ethic means nothing if your body can't handle your fast pace. Being active also doesn't mean you need to become a fitness guru (I mean, unless you want to). I often convince myself that in order to be healthy, I need to change everything about my life—I need to go to the gym for two hours every day and stop eating yummy food. But that's not the case. Making small changes in order to live a healthier lifestyle can make a big difference. Here are a few ideas.

1 STRETCH IN THE MORNINGS

I'm going to be honest: most of my mornings begin in an extreme state of panic because I pressed snooze too many times and now I need to brush my teeth while somehow eating cereal if I'm going to make it to my meeting on time. I've never really tasted the original flavor of Cheerios. But the few times I have woken up on time and taken a few minutes to stretch, it's made a huge difference in my day. Not only do I feel more energized and ready to take on the day, but I also don't move like a ninety-year-old grandma. Who would have thought?!

2 DON'T TAKE THE EASY WAY

Throughout your day, take the stairs instead of an escalator (I think you've heard this before), walk to your destination instead of driving, get up to change the channel instead of using the remote, and when you're getting ready to go out, dance like no one is watching.

3 DON'T BE SO HARD ON YOURSELF

Sometimes I stop eating all my favorite foods in an attempt to be healthy. But after a few days I cave and binge-eat all the extra-buttery popcorn. It's not a good look. You don't need to cut out your favorite foods completely; you just need to eat things in moderation. If you really want some popcorn, have the popcorn, but make yourself a deal. While the popcorn is popping, do some jumping jacks, and instead of extra butter, settle for regular.

4 DRINK WATER

I don't think there's ever been a day in the history of my life, except for maybe when I needed to get an ultrasound, when I've had eight glasses of water. That's just so much water. Also, there are way more delicious things to drink! But drinking water has so many benefits that it's literally stupid not to just do it. One of the ways I've learned to drink more water is to pay attention to my glass while I drink it. I know that may sound silly, but what I noticed is that when I drink water it's ONLY because I'm thirsty, and so I take a few sips and am done with it. I never actually look at my glass and commit to finishing it. Talk about first-world privilege. So now when I'm drinking water, I don't put the glass down or walk away until I finish the glass. Sometimes that even means telling myself, "Okay, three more big gulps and then you can leave," as if I'm a four-year-old child. For example, earlier today I told myself that I wasn't allowed to enter my apartment from the hallway unless I finished the water in my bottle. I stood there in the hallway guzzling water for five minutes.

Another great life hack: drink a glass of water every time you post on Instagram (or your favorite social media platform). Some of you will be drinking fifteen glasses a day, which is a good indicator that you should slow your roll. If you're overflowing, you'll know how our timelines feel.

When I was on tour I was in great shape. My show involved a lot of dancing, which helped build my stamina, and I was getting a lot more done in a day because my body could keep up with my mental hustle. I'd

**BEING ACTIVE
HAS NOTHING TO DO WITH
BEING SEXY,
SCULPTING A SIX-PACK,
OR FITTING INTO
A SMALLER SIZE. IT'S ABOUT
MAKING SURE
YOUR BODY CAN KEEP UP
WITH YOUR HUSTLE.**

go to rehearsals, do four or five interviews, carry out a sound check, go for a meet-and-greet, perform a show, and then hop on a plane and do it all again the next day. When I'm not in shape, I walk up the stairs to my office and feel like I need to take a nap to recover.

On tour I also drank a lot of water because (a) it was a nervous habit and (b) during every costume change I would guzzle water to cool myself down. It wasn't until the tour was over that I realized I hadn't gotten a single pimple on my face in two months of traveling. H_2O for the win!

I know it can be hard, but it's important to be active and healthy. Aging is inevitable and poor health will catch up to you very quickly. A Bawse knows the importance of creating a positive environment for the mind, heart, and soul. You can't have a happy mind if you have an unhappy body; it just doesn't work. They would fight and break up. You don't want your body sleeping on the sofa, do you? I didn't think so.

Hydrate

If you struggle to drink water, get up now and grab a glass of water. Finish the entire glass before you turn the page. Let the good habit begin!

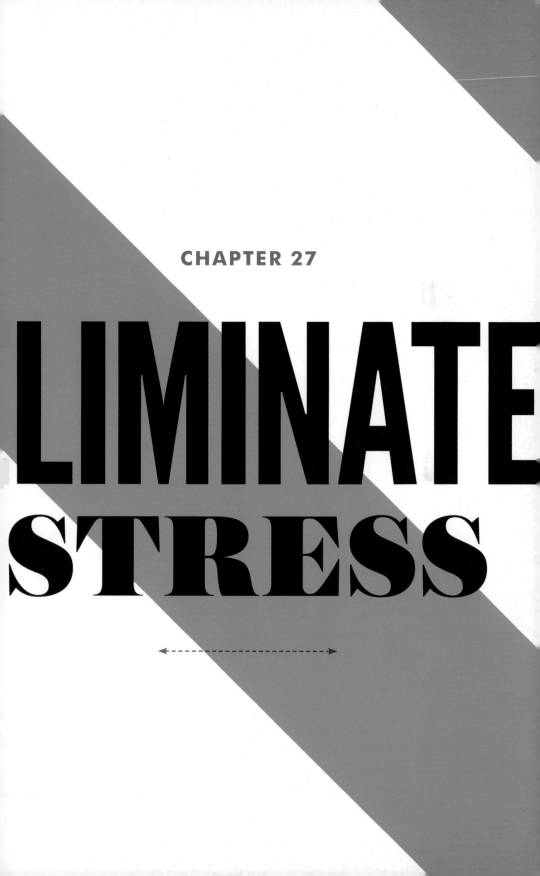

CHAPTER 27

ELIMINATE STRESS

SO THERE I AM,

on the final lap, driving full speed ahead with my tongue hanging out. My green skin is glowing with adrenaline as I pass Luigi. Sorry, dude, there's only room for one adorable green character on the road, and that's me, Yoshi. I make a sharp left turn and, before I can dodge it, my tires drive over a banana peel, causing me to spin out. UGH! You stupid little banana! Luigi and all his friends pass me. I finally stop spinning and continue racing full speed ahead until my kart slips on an oil spill and I spin out yet again. This time I career off the track into the abyss. I fall into tenth, eleventh, and now twelfth place, until finally the race ends without me crossing the finish line. I didn't reach my destination.

Life is sort of like *Mario Kart,* and every day we play a different level. We wake up and race through the day, trying to reach the final destination, but we're bombarded by little nuisances at every turn. In *Mario Kart* these nuisances are banana peels, oil spills, shells, hidden bombs, and bouncing fireballs. In real life (not to imply you're not real, Mario; I'm not trying to throw shade at you like that, bro), these nuisances can include anything from a dead phone battery to not having a hair tie when you need one the most to a completely full parking lot outside the building where your next meeting is. Although these things all seem minor, when you add them up they can throw a huge monkey wrench into your day.

I am a very detailed-oriented person. In fact, sometimes I'm a little *too* detail-oriented and I drive my team crazy. But that's because I understand that avoiding tiny little mishaps throughout the day will make a huge difference in my productivity. I've had days where my schedule consists of creating a video, doing three interviews, attending a meeting, and participating in a conference call, all while having a positive attitude. The last thing I need on a day like that is to have my phone die on me so I can't look up an address. Or not have a hair tie while I'm trying to eat, resulting in me swallowing a chunk of my own hair. Or, most commonly, not be able to find parking near my next meeting, which I'm already running late for. These are all avoidable, unnecessary stresses that eat away at your soul and consume energy. Think of what you could do with just a little extra energy every day. So, how do you avoid these little banana peels throughout your day? You take preventive measures to ensure that the banana peels you slipped on today are tossed into the compost for tomorrow. (Notice I said compost and not trash. How Mother Nature of me.)

If I've had a super-frustrating day, before I call it a night I will take a moment to sit down and list all the stresses I encountered throughout my day. No stress is too little or whiny or silly to go on the list. It's my day, my stress, and my productivity that's been affected, so I can put whatever I want on the list. If the wind kept blowing my hair and causing it to stick to my lip gloss, then "wind" is absolutely going on there. Here's an example of a list I've made:

- My stupid phone died at noon.
- My lips were dry and I felt unsexy.
- I couldn't find parking.
- I was starving.

Putting all the challenges in my day on paper makes it much easier to identify and tackle them one by one. The best plan of attack? Be prepared.

Looking at the list, I realized that parking has always been a huge stress for me, mostly because I suck at it. Now, whenever I have to drive to a meeting, I tell my assistant to list parking options in my iCal alongside the event details. That way I'll know if the building has a parking lot, where to go if it's full, and if street parking is available. Parking panic? Solved.

The day after I made that list, I bought three iPhone chargers—one for my car, one for my backpack, and one for my washroom. In fact, in almost every outlet of my apartment you can find an iPhone charger because nothing is more annoying than trying to turn on a dead iPhone. These days, resurrecting a dead phone is like bringing Jon Snow back to life: it takes *forever*. (Also, if that was a *Game of Thrones* spoiler for you, then you have questionable priorities.) Dead phone? Solved. Next up: dry lips.

If I'm in the middle of a meeting and my lips are dry, I literally cannot focus on anything that is happening because I'm positive everyone is staring at my lips and wondering how I've survived twenty-eight years with sandpaper on my face. So, in addition to the iPhone chargers, the next day

I bought three ChapSticks: one for my backpack, one for my car, and one for my night table. Parched lips? Solved.

For someone who loves food so much, I am the worst eater ever. On a super-busy day I will actually forget to eat. Literally forget. I am so focused when it comes to completing my work that I will subconsciously tune out the little voice coming from my stomach, begging me to feed it. I will become numb to hunger pains, and it's not until I start feeling faint that I remember that I didn't eat breakfast. That's usually around 7:00 P.M. Thus I placed granola bars in all the same strategic places I have my chargers and ChapSticks. I've started to pre-pack a breakfast and leave it at the front door. A bag of cereal, an apple, and a bottle of water can go a *long* way. Hunger games? Solved.

These are all examples of very simple fixes that required only two things: recognition and problem-solving. So often we deal with little issues throughout the day, get frustrated, and then do nothing to solve them but curse out loud. That's not productive. I have worked very hard to train myself to PROBLEM-SOLVE instead of becoming frustrated. I've learned that frustration will not manifest a phone charger or ChapStick no matter how much I yell and scream.

Aside from implementing fixes to small problems, it's important to also eliminate stress around larger events and recurring tasks. I travel a lot, and that can either be pleasant or horrible. There's seldom a middle ground. As you can imagine, every time I travel there are many things that get added to my stress list. By now, I've identified the things that vastly improve my travel experience, none of which require more than a little time and effort:

- Confirming my vegetarian meal. They will always screw this up. You must do it online AND call the airline to confirm. It's basically rocket science for them.

- Securing a window seat on the right side of the plane. I have neck issues that are more prominent on the left side of my neck, so leaning my head to the left gives me migraines.

- Bringing my own shawl. I am always freezing with just the blanket they provide and never get any work done because I'm trying not to die of frostbite.

- Prepping for the immigration card. I have a picture of my passport saved in a secure folder on my phone so that I can easily fill these out. Also, I always make sure I have a pen easily accessible in my backpack.

The above guidelines are now routine. You may think, "Okay, really, Lilly? The right side of the plane?" But hey, why not make little changes that make a difference to you? Every little bit of stress you eliminate contributes to a more productive day. That's not being a diva; it's placing yourself in a situation that allows you to be in optimal form.

Another example of being proactive: having meetings after recurring events to review how things went. If you're going to be with the same team for a long time, you need to work together to make sure things go smoother and smoother each time. When I was on tour, the cast and crew and I would have a debriefing after every single show, from the very first show to the thirty-first show. Yes, we had a debriefing just for fun after the last show (we're obsessed). We would discuss every technical error or mishap in choreography and come up with a solution right then and there. Sometimes the solution was complicated and required a change in music, and other times the solution was as minor as someone moving slightly to the left. Everyone communicated their issues and we all worked on solutions. The result was a cleaner show every single time.

The next time you're in a stressful situation, instead of becoming flustered and frustrated, take a deep breath and ask yourself, "What can I change next time to avoid this situation?" And then proactively take steps to implement a solution. We only have twenty-four hours to finish today's level of *Mario Kart,* and we need to maximize our ability to get things done. After all, we have as many hours in the day as Beyoncé, but we're at a disadvantage already, because we're not Beyoncé. Just kidding! You're just as capable as Beyoncé! Yeah, I said that.

I can see Luigi trembling in his boots already.

Apply It

List two things that stressed you out this week and come up with solutions to eliminate them.

1. _____

2. _____

CHAPTER 28

MOLD YOUR FAILURE

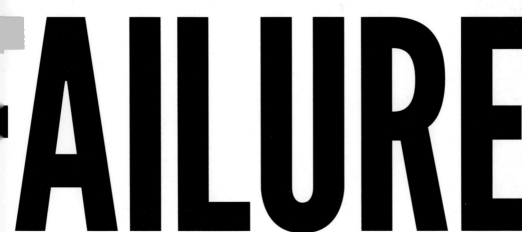

MY OMELETS ALWAYS

turn into scrambled eggs. I start off with confidence as my eggs spread perfectly across the pan in a magnificent circle. Every single time I think, "OMG, am I an Iron Chef?" As I order a chef's hat off Amazon with one hand, I use the other hand to flip my omelet. One hundred percent of the time I perform this move prematurely and my omelet breaks into at least three pieces. After staring at my failure for five seconds (and attempting to cancel my Amazon order), I grab my spatula and break the eggs into even more pieces. I like scrambled eggs better anyway.

Failure doesn't necessarily mean the end of an idea or project. When things don't go the way we anticipate, it's easy to feel like we have to start over, but that's not always the case. Just because one door has closed, it doesn't mean it can't be knocked down or forced back open. I know the quote goes "When one door closes, another opens." But why didn't anyone ever try opening the closed door? Or better yet, finding a back door? I just feel like that quote doesn't factor in effort or imagination or logic. A Bawse knows that, yes, sometimes failure does indeed mean starting over. But a Bawse also knows that other times failure can be molded into unexpected success.

In December 2015, I was working on my "12 Collaborations of Christmas," a series I do every year that consists of twelve high-profile collaborations with a holiday theme. Each year I try to make the series bigger and better (obviously, like a Bawse), and I reach out to people who excite me, so that they can excite my audience as well. I've worked with people like Stephanie McMahon, Adam Devine, Russell Peters, and Gina Rodriguez. That year I decided to reach out to one of my biggest inspirations, an A-list movie actress, whom I adore. I had a good feeling about it, because she had a film set to release during the holiday season. You see, when another artist has a new project coming out, it's easier to confirm a collaboration because there's an opportunity for cross-promotion. Apparently there was an event being held in New York City in two weeks that was aimed toward marketing her upcoming film. Part of the marketing plan was to highlight influential women through a variety of media, including online content. Ding, ding, ding! Hello, I am a creator of online content, how may I help you?

My team set up a call for me to pitch an idea for a collaboration. I came up with a creative challenge called the "#GirlLove Challenge." The idea was to make a game out of spitting rapid-fire compliments at pictures of influential women and encourage viewers to do the same. Very simple and effective. To my great joy, my idea was well received, and I was all set to fly to New York to shoot the video in just a few days. I was over the moon. And not just our moon. Jupiter's moons. All sixty-seven of them.

Two days before I was supposed to take off, I still didn't have a flight booked. It made me feel unsettled. It's cool, though, I thought. This is how L.A. functions, *super*-last-minute. I continued ironing out the details of my #GirlLove Challenge until my manager called me with some bad news. For

whatever reason, the shoot wasn't going to happen anymore. I wasn't going to New York and I wasn't going to collaborate with one of my biggest inspirations. Just like that. In a matter of minutes, everything fell apart. I was absolutely heartbroken.

For a whole day I walked around like a zombie, completely unmotivated and disappointed. I loved the #GirlLove Challenge idea so much, and I was bummed that it wouldn't happen. I complained and ranted and then finally tired myself out and went to bed. While lying there, unable to sleep, I had a spontaneous

I KNOW THE QUOTE GOES 'WHEN ONE DOOR CLOSES ANOTHER OPENS.' BUT WHY DIDN'T ANYONE EVER TRY OPENING THE CLOSED DOOR?

thought: What if I didn't need to collaborate with a movie star to do the challenge? What if I stopped focusing on the person I couldn't meet with and started thinking about all the people I did have access to? After all, I believed in the *idea* more than anything! Right then and there, I sent a voice note to my management saying that the #GirlLove Challenge would happen, regardless, and I would need their help. I was going to pry the door back open.

Over the next week I contacted every influential woman I knew, from Grace Helbig to Shay Mitchell, and got them to send me a clip complimenting another woman, aka the #GirlLove Challenge. Instead of focusing the whole thing around an upcoming movie, I focused on my channel's demographic and pivoted the challenge toward making a positive difference for my large female audience. I released the video, featuring eighteen influential women, as one of my Christmas collaborations—and the response was overwhelming. Countless media outlets picked up the video, and it reached the likes of Tyra Banks and Priyanka Chopra (to name a few), who each tweeted about it and took part in the challenge. The #GirlLove became a global phenomenon—young girls across the globe were complimenting each other on social media using the hashtag #GirlLove.

After all the hype died down, which it eventually did, I thought the #GirlLove Challenge would die too. It might become a once-upon-a-time viral hit. However, the video birthed a passion within me, and in 2016 I hired a team and launched #GirlLove as a full-fledged social campaign. Today, as I write this, #GirlLove has a complete social strategy and is an episodic series on my channel. It got me inside the White House to discuss women's issues with Michelle Obama and recently allowed me to travel to Kenya to learn more about women's education in the Maasai community. Furthermore, a #GirlLove rafiki bracelet was created in partnership with

ME to WE (an amazing organization—Google them) and the proceeds are going toward giving Kenyan girls scholarships to attend secondary school. I also held a workshop in Singapore to teach young girls how to spread #GirlLove, and the venue was completely sold out. All of this happened because my collaboration didn't work out. Every success that #GirlLove has is a direct result of molding the broken pieces of a previous failure.

In most negative situations in life, you can create a positive outcome if you just look hard enough. Aside from the #GirlLove Challenge, there is a much greater example from my life in which I took something not so great and made it great. When people ask me what I'm most grateful for in life, they get confused when I reply, "Depression." I started making YouTube videos in 2010 because I was trying to make myself happy and escape depression. I thought if I could make others laugh, then I could also make myself laugh. My dedication to YouTube was me self-medicating; it was a pick-me-up, a distraction, and a goal to work toward. To this day, depression is the worst feeling I've ever encountered in my life. It was heart-wrenchingly painful. Everything I have today—every video, success, and opportunity—is the direct result of taking that pain and turning it into something positive: comedy. I'll never have to take a pottery class because I've already molded the most difficult thing: my life.

To take failure and turn it on its head, to make something unexpected out of it, is a beautiful thing. I could have abandoned the #GirlLove Challenge. I could have let my depression take me down a path that led nowhere. But instead I decided to get my hands dirty with some Play-Doh and create something new. Often we're too busy being disappointed or upset to recognize that the tools we need to create a new masterpiece are right in front of us. They just require a little rearranging and assembly. Don't let disappointment blind you to potential. Roll up your sleeves, use your creativity as glue, and mold your success.

CHAPTER 29

CLIMB
ANOTHER
LADDER

MY LIMO PULLS UP

and the driver walks around to open the door for me. As soon as I step on the red carpet, my fans go crazy and start chanting my name. Cameras are flashing and my security is surrounding me. I'm about to walk into the premiere of my very own movie, *A Trip to Unicorn Island,* a documentary that follows me on my world tour. It's taking place at the prestigious Chinese Theatre in Los Angeles. The entire street is shut down for my event. The film is a hit and I have a blast at the afterparty. People are congratulating me left, right, and center. Mama, I've made it.

Fast-forward to two days later and I'm nervously driving around a studio, completely lost, already two minutes late. I park somewhere random and speed-walk toward the closest person I see to ask for directions. They have no clue. I find someone else and they proceed to draw me a map on a pamphlet with a dying pen. I race left, then right, then left again, trying desperately to follow these chicken-scratch directions. Finally I find the building and walk into my audition. I sit down in a small room with a water fountain and two other people. No one even looks at me. Eventually a woman calls my name and I follow her into an even smaller room. She riffles through some paperwork without giving me a proper look and says, "Do you have your headshot?" Confused, I reply, "Um, my agent should have sent all my information." She looks up at me and says, "Oh, sorry. Found it. Lilly, right?" Yup. That's me. I do the audition and within 120 seconds I'm back out the door, struggling to find my car. I am a nobody.

These two experiences are my life in a nutshell. Within forty-eight hours I go from being a superstar to "Lilly, right?" Sometimes it's even within the same day. In the digital space I'm considered a star, but in Hollywood I'm just another person waiting to audition. I've learned that success in one area of your life doesn't guarantee or entitle you to success in another. That's why A-list celebrities have relationship problems and the most popular kids in school may not have the best grades. Just because you've climbed one ladder doesn't mean you won't have to start from the bottom of another ladder.

When I decided to try getting into TV and film, it took me a while to get used to the audition process. I come from a world where I write, shoot, edit, and release my own content. I make the rules and I know what I want. When I walk into an audition, I have one sentence describing the character I'm supposed to play and a roomful of people watching me critically. It's the perfect atmosphere to ensure that you DON'T do your best. But just like I earned my stripes on YouTube, I knew I would have to start from the bottom of the Hollywood ladder. My career in the digital space gives me a slight advantage because I have a good agency repping me, but regardless of that, I'm still out there auditioning for two-line cameos in movies. I'm at the top of one ladder and at the bottom of another.

Is it frustrating? Of course. I'm doing a diagonal split across two ladders and my legs hurt. So why do I do it? Because I don't want my pride to get in the way of achieving everything I want. The last thing I want is for my ego to prevent me from thinking I shouldn't have to earn something. If I want to expand my brand and skill set, which I do, then I need to earn it, which I will.

It's also a matter of respecting a different ladder and everyone on it. The climb up any ladder teaches you lessons and provides you with the necessary experiences. If I went from the top of my current ladder to the top of another ladder, I would have no clue what was below me. I would be inexperienced and probably fall to my death. In the same way, someone from another industry who jumps onto my ladder shouldn't expect to be on top. With all due respect, if you're going to stand beside me on the ladder I'm on and have no idea what a YouTube annotation is, that's problematic.

There are many examples of people who have climbed multiple ladders and will probably continue to do so. The Rock (have I mentioned him before in this book?) went from being a pro wrestler to being a successful actor. That's two ladders. He didn't start his acting career as the world's most-paid actor; he earned that title by climbing his way up. Drake went from acting to music. That's two ladders as well. Justin Timberlake did the exact opposite and went from music to acting and back again. There is no all-access pass. No matter who you are, there is going to be something you want to do that will require you to start from the bottom. That shouldn't scare you because you're a Bawse and you thrive on challenges. You don't feel entitled to success—you feel empowered to earn it. So earn it, again and again.

OUT OF THE BLUE

2010 It's such a weird sensation to feel unimportant and invisible, and yet also feel like every person in the world is staring at you. I feel like there's a huge neon sign above my head that reads "depressed" or "worthless." I want to stay in my room all day, sitting in the dark, locked away from the world. That's where I feel safest, although, to be honest, I'm the least safe person in my life.

When I'm walking down the street, everyone is looking at me. I might not see them looking at me, but I know they are. My brain is telling me they are. My darkness is an aura that does not go unnoticed. I hate when they look at me and I wish they would leave me alone, because I'm not proud of the person they see. I'm so uncomfortable in public and around people. I look down nervously and wring my hands in my pocket, counting down the seconds until I can be alone again, until I can hide again.

The only sanctuary I have is at the temple. I go there every day and sit in the back, as far away from everyone else as possible. But I still feel as if everyone is looking at me. Why wouldn't they? I radiate sadness.

When I get home, I struggle to look in the mirror because I don't want to face myself. I don't know what to say to my reflection. We haven't been friends for a while now. I look away and swallow the reality that tomorrow will be just like today, another day filled with people staring at me. I am dreading it.

2015 It's such an exhilarating sensation to feel so loved and have so many people staring at you. I see a huge sign with flashing lights outside the venue that reads "Lilly Singh's *A Trip to Unicorn Island*—SOLD OUT." I know tonight is going to be magical. I want to be on tour forever, sitting in my dressing room, ready to take on another city. I feel my best when I'm onstage, and to be honest, it's where I *am* my best.

I pace back and forth backstage, fired up, ready to put on the show of a lifetime. My stride is strong and full of power. My chin is up, my head is high, and my body is ready. I am so happy.

When I walk onto the stage, everyone is on their feet, screaming with excitement, looking at me. It doesn't just FEEL like they're looking at me, I can SEE them looking at me, and it feels magnificent. When I'm performing, my charisma *can't* go unnoticed. I'm floating, with complete confidence, from one side of the stage to another. I feel comfortable here, with all eyes on me. And when I have to leave this stage, I'll be counting down the seconds until I return.

I take a long look at myself in the mirror before and after each show. My reflection is of Superwoman. I look her right in the eyes and have a conversation with her, telling her how proud I am of her. She's my best friend. I reluctantly pull myself away from the mirror and begin taking my costume off.

I feel blessed that tomorrow is another show and I get to live this reality again. I am living for it.

PART 3
MAKE HEADS TURN

A Bawse doesn't blend into a crowd—they stand out. In this section you'll learn how to make people pay attention to you, how to interact with others effectively, how to have an unforgettable presence, and how to use your deeper understanding of who you are to be the best possible version of yourself. There are 7 billion people on the planet. That's 14 billion socks to knock off.

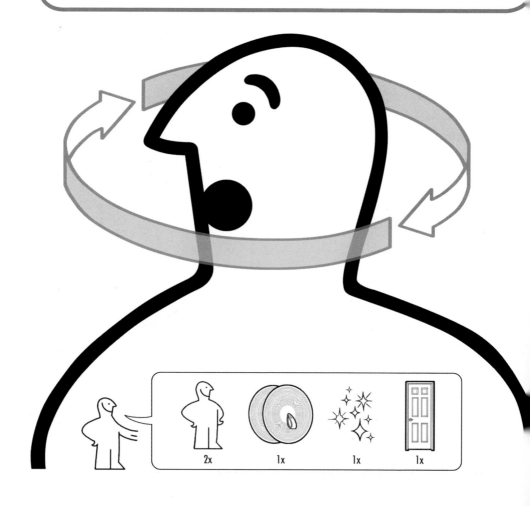

CHAPTER 30

YOU ARE NOT A
PARKING
TICKET

<----------------------->

SINCE BIRTH

I'm sure you've heard the magical words "you're special" repeated by your parents, your teachers, and your favorite children's TV show host. I grew up watching Barney, that giant purple dinosaur who was always smiling and friendly. Now that I think about it, maybe he was a little too smiley. Then again, Selena Gomez and Demi Lovato were on the show as toddlers, so I guess that would make me smile nonstop too. This purple friend of mine would tell me on a daily basis how special I was. And how special my friends were. And my classmates. And my neighbors (even though they would put their excess garbage bags on our driveway because they exceeded the limit). Everyone was special! Well, I'm here to tell you two things: (1) you're special and (2) you're not special.

You're special because you are a unique individual possessing a set of characteristics that no one else in the world has. Even if you have an identical twin born four minutes after you (in which case you should probably hug your mother's uterus on a daily basis), there is still no one in the world exactly like you—and that makes you special. But that specialness goes away if you do not do anything with your unique characteristics. Harry Potter is special because he is a powerful wizard and uses his powers for good. Imagine if he discovered his powers, got accepted into Hogwarts, and then decided, "Nah, I'm good. I'm just going to continue living under these stairs, not using my powers, and let these next four books be a major flop. Sorry, J. K. Rowling, no bestsellers for you!"

Millennials in particular have been raised in an environment that validates them left and right and makes them feel entitled to success and great things. Instead of working hard to achieve success, some of them have grown up under the illusion that success should automatically be granted to them. I believe there are a few reasons for this. First, social media has made it easy to feel special for no reason at all. If you can sign into Tumblr, then you deserve to feel special—and look, there's a quote right there to reassure you, you queen. If you ever feel like you're not accomplishing enough, that's okay! Your last Instagram picture got seventy likes! Retweets, double taps, reblogs, and followers are all modern-day forms of validation. Today an Instagram picture of you at the gym that gets a lot of likes is more validating than the actual benefits of going to the gym. Who needs health and muscles when I got double taps?! That's the real win! And . . . that's wack.

Second, now more than ever, there are ten thousand people online—and in real life—telling you how to raise your kids: feed them organic foods, tell them you love them four times a day, and hug them with both arms every half hour so they can feel your warmth. I'm not a parent, so I'm not going to comment too much on raising kids. But I will say that I have witnessed firsthand the effects of parents who too readily validate their children and everything they do.

I once had a friend who was awesome. He was a truly nice guy—very polite and pleasant to be around. Over time I noticed that he had one characteristic that I didn't particularly enjoy, and that was his sense of entitlement. During an argument, he would assume that it was everyone's job to nurture his feelings and make them a priority. If his accomplishments were not celebrated to the extreme, he would feel disrespected. If he made plans and they didn't go exactly the way he wanted, he would become enraged. I didn't understand why he had this entitlement complex until I met his family. Within moments it was clear that he had grown up surrounded by constant validation. Every sentence was praise for their godlike son, who was the pride and joy of the entire human race. Every single accomplishment, no matter how big or small, garnered celebratory cake, gifts, and a roundtable discussion about how great my friend was. Within an hour I was drowning in a pool of validation. And it wasn't a pleasant pool with a swim-up bar and cute floaties, but rather quite concerning. I now understood why my friend acted the way he did. He'd been raised as the king of the family and thus believed he should be treated like a king in all other situations. Well, what a harsh reality he is going to face in life.

A Bawse knows that if they're going to feel validated, it should happen only when they accomplish goals or contribute to society. It's so easy to fall into the trap of feeling special for no reason, especially since validation feels so good. A few years ago I was asked to host VidCon, a huge convention that features YouTube creators and thousands and thousands of fans.

In other words, it's three days of wonderful chaos and screaming as fans try to sneak into hotel rooms, take selfies with their favorite creators, and get various parts of their bodies autographed.

Now, as you know, I take performing very seriously. No matter how big or small an event is, I want to ensure I do the best possible job, and so I'm constantly asking about talking points, production, and mic cues. Moments before I went on the VidCon stage, I approached the show producer to confirm everything that was going to happen during my segment. His response was, "Honestly, you're Superwoman and they're going to cheer and go crazy for you regardless of what happens." You might think that would have made me feel special, but in truth I felt my entire soul crushed under the weight of his validation. I value the performing arts and I work hard to create meaningful, funny content. I never want to get cheers on a stage simply for standing there like a bag of bones.

I've gotten the same type of validation in the comments section of my videos. I've read comments that say, "You are the funniest person in the world and the best human being ever and everyone else sucks compared to you!" Does that mean I should walk around thinking I'm the funniest person on the planet? God, no. That's stupid, because Amy Schumer exists on the planet. Feeling validated from over-the-top positive comments is the same thing as getting discouraged by over-the-top negative comments. I try to stay immune to both, even though validation feels great. Sometimes when I ask my audience what they want to see in the next video, I'll get responses like, "You could make a whole video just sitting and saying nothing and we'd still watch it!" But I would rather strangle myself with my hair than make that video. (Strangling myself with my hair, by the way, is very possible. My cousins used to do it to me all the time when I was younger. It was playful, though. Don't call the cops.) I never want to let my own entitlement get in the way of my content. That's a slippery slope and I choose not to go skiing. I treat feedback the way teachers treat standardized tests: you cut off the highest and lowest outliers and don't let them impact the overall score. The greatest feedback and worst feedback are both dangerous in their own way.

On that point, one of the biggest dangers of being easily validated is the fact that validation is a major threat to one's ambition and hustle. When you have a list of ten goals and people throw you parties after you've finished three of them, that can make you feel like maybe the other seven goals aren't that important. Or, you know what? I'll get to them later, after all these celebratory events being held in my honor are over. Validation is temporary, and a Bawse thinks long-term.

Don't get me wrong, you should definitely celebrate when you accomplish something great. Celebrating yourself is an important part of loving yourself. But be aware of getting validated without reason or too often, because an overly comfortable environment is not one in which hustle thrives. I'm confident that one of the reasons my hustle is so raging is that my mother keeps her validations locked away in a chest that she only occasionally opens. I can call and tell her about the biggest deal I just signed and she will respond by saying, "That's really good." That's it. She's happy and proud, but there's no need to throw me a parade every time I do something. That helps me keep my goals in perspective and not get sidetracked by the euphoria of glory.

Nice comments on Instagram, compliments in real life, and celebratory dinners can all be great. They mean your friends and family care about you. But do not let these gestures cloud your sense of reality and affect *why* you do what you do—or worse, let them convince you that you don't need to do anything else.

If you're reading this and feeling offended, I'm going to ask you to take a deep breath and let your guard down. Don't close this book and go watch *Barney* videos on YouTube to make yourself feel better. It's a beautiful thing to let achievements make you feel good, rather than praise and other fluffy things. You're not a parking ticket. Don't get so easily validated.

Participation ribbons are for country fairs, not life. You don't get one for being born.

CHAPTER 31

PROTECT YOUR VISION

IN SEX EDUCATION CLASS

I learned that when a man and woman have intercourse, the woman can become impregnated and carry a child in her belly for nine months. Me, on the other hand, I have many kids, but I didn't have intercourse to create them. I have just the kids with none of the action. That's why I drink vodka on Tuesdays.

Recently I've learned that there are other ways to have children, or at least, in my opinion, the fulfillment that comes from having kids. I often tell my mom that she doesn't need to keep asking me about grandkids because I've given birth to so many brain babies. In fact, you're holding one right now: this book. Be sure to support the spine! Like I would with a newborn, I nurture my ideas, help them grow, and hope that one day they will become something great. When my ideas are young and can barely walk on their own, they keep me up at night. Similarly, when my ideas grow old, I realize I can't hold on to them anymore and need to let them go.

Good parents have an innate desire to protect their children, and I have that same instinct when it comes to my brain babies. Our children are exposed to so many negative influences. The kids at school might do drugs, the media encourages a superficial lifestyle, and then there's always that one annoying uncle at parties who tries to give your baby soft drinks just to shut them up. Just the same, my brain baby is out there in the cruel world, susceptible to bad influences, and it's up to me to make sure I protect it.

In 2014, I woke up one morning and felt nauseated. I ran to the bathroom and puked my guts out, looked up at the mirror, and knew this was morning sickness. Also, I'm totally kidding and that didn't happen, BUT I did wake up feeling a strange sensation. The night before had been wild! I'd been hosting a dance competition and the event was sold out. So many of my supporters had come to see me emcee, which was sweet since, really, I would be onstage only a few seconds at a time. I remember standing on the side of the stage, listening to the crowd, and then suddenly feeling a jolt in my heart. In that moment I really wished I could be onstage for the entire show, connect with the audience, and do things my way. For years I had been hosting, doing fifteen-minute stand-up routines or making short speeches, and I suddenly didn't want that anymore. I wanted my own show. Fast-forward to the next morning: I woke up feeling inspired and knew that I had been impregnated with a brain baby.

For the next year or so, I worked on my very first world tour, called *A Trip to Unicorn Island*. Like most new mothers, I had no idea what the hell I was doing, but I knew I loved this baby with all my heart. I wanted to feed it organic fruits and use only natural baby products. Whenever I met someone new, I pulled out my phone to show them pictures of my tour creative because it was growing up so fast. My Facebook feed was filled with sentimental posts about my tour. I was *that* mother.

After several late nights filled with pizza and alcohol (the good thing about brain babies is that drinking may actually have a positive impact on them, unlike real human babies, who are selfish and demanding, kicking you all up in your uterus—just saying), I had a vision of how I wanted this show to look. I had ideas for everything, from the marketing to the costumes to the merchandise being sold. Now, when people embark on their first tour it's usually small, often within a particular region of the globe, and the crew is minimal. But I wanted my show to be a WORLD TOUR that traveled across the planet, was theatrical in nature, and was above and beyond anything I'd ever done. It came as no surprise when my manager called me and said the production company had crunched all the numbers and had some concerns. From that point on, meetings and phone calls were filled with various obstacles that threatened my vision: finances, logistics, legalities, and a bunch of other ridiculous things, like gravity. Pffft. Whatever, gravity. You're not the boss of me!

One of the major sticking points was the number of dancers that would be on tour with me. I envisioned eight but was told that we could only afford four. Over and over again I was told I needed to confirm four dancers or else the tour would not be financially viable. Here's the thing, though: with four dancers, it wouldn't be my tour, the one I had in my head. It would be my team's tour, my financial advisor's tour, but not *my* tour—and that wasn't okay with me. I signed off on taking full financial responsibility for eight dancers.

I finally had my eight dancers confirmed, but this was just the first of many battles I would fight. I went back and forth with the costume designer, not budging on what I wanted because I had a very specific vision in my mind. She kept coming to me with reasons why my vision wouldn't be possible to execute, but I was adamant. My dancers were to be the gate-keepers of Unicorn Island, and they had to look perfect. My baby would not wear an ugly onesie! My baby had to wear a cute, fluffy outfit so I could take pictures of it and plaster those pictures on the Internet. That's what motherhood is about!

After months of protecting my baby with invisible boxing gloves, the time finally came to start the tour. Little did I know that the actual journey across the planet would be filled with unforeseen threats to my vision. In India, some of my jokes had to be altered due to legalities and cultural appropriateness. In Perth, Australia, the size of the stage was a third of our minimum requirement. In Dubai, the staff continuously interrupted my show and the security allowed fans to run onstage during my set. But I'm a mother, and mothers do not give up when it comes to protecting their young, so time and time again I tried my best to find a solution. I just wanted my baby to shine and make a difference in the world.

Now, this all sounds ideal and magical in some sense, but a Bawse understands that there is a cost to protecting your vision. With dancers and costumes, I took on financial risk. With stage dimensions and venue restrictions, the dancers would have to rearrange formations to accommodate the changes. With logistics and scheduling, I sacrificed the amount of time I had to sleep. When it comes to protecting your vision, there will always be some cost, and you need to be prepared to deal with it. More often than not, the cost will be a huge amount of work. If you want things a certain way, then you better be on the front lines of the battle with a suit of armor, ready to protect your brain baby.

The next time you have an idea, recognize that your idea is your baby and if you parent it well, it will grow up to be a wonderful event, product, or campaign. Your baby can change the world, but first you must make a promise to protect it. You should always welcome feedback and take into account suggestions that may help your baby in a positive way, BUT if you ever hear that little voice in your head screaming in protest, you should stick to your guns.

Welcome to parenthood. You should go to a hardware store right now and buy some childproof locks (and earplugs), because that's what parenting is all about. That and getting peed on while changing diapers. Dang, I guess gravity really does exist.

"

GOOD PARENTS HAVE AN INNATE DESIRE TO PROTECT THEIR CHILDREN, AND I HAVE THAT SAME INSTINCT WHEN IT COMES TO MY BRAIN BABIES.

"

CHAPTER 32

BE THE DUMBEST

SNOOP DOGG

has taught me a lot of valuable lessons in life. For starters, he taught me that you can spell animal names however you want, so if you feel like repeating a letter, don't let anyone stop you. Second, if something is hot, drop it. And last, I'm beautiful and he just wanted me to know. I learned all these things through Snoop Dogg's iconic music, but it was during a YouTube creator summit he was speaking at that I ended up learning the most. He was participating in a panel about staying relevant in the industry and I was sitting on the edge of my seat trying to soak in all the wisdom. He said a lot of really great things that day, but one thing in particular stood out to me. When asked how he's been able to have such a long, successful career, Snoop Dogg replied: "I'm the dumbest person on my team and that's how I do it."

From a young age we're always taught to be the best, the fastest, and the smartest. You don't aim for second place in a race, nor do you compete in a spelling bee hoping someone else is a better speller than you. That said, a Bawse knows that in certain situations, it's beneficial to be the dumbest person in the room. Surrounding yourself with people who are more experienced and knowledgeable than you are is a great way to step outside your comfort zone and continue to learn and grow.

When it comes to my team, I'm the talent. This means that it's my job to be in front of the camera, onstage, or in a studio. Although I may be good at entertaining the masses, I wouldn't be where I am if it weren't for a number of other people who are really good at their jobs. I'm good at telling jokes, but my manager is better than me at strategizing my overall career. Performing in front of 18,000 people is no problem for me, but when it comes to the legalities of that performance, my lawyer is much more knowledgeable than me. The stories and lessons in this book are my brain babies, but without my editor you wouldn't be able to read my incorrectly spelled sentences (sometimes not even autocorrect can save you). When it comes to my team, I'm the best at doing what I'm supposed to do, but I'm the absolute dumbest when it comes to everything else. And I wouldn't want it any other way. It's like we're all holding our own paddle, one that no one else knows how to handle, and we're rowing in unison.

Being the dumbest person on your team doesn't make you a stupid person; it means you're smart enough to select people to work with that you can learn from. It also means checking your ego and being okay with the fact that you aren't the best at something. When I'm in a meeting with my team, every member has something to contribute to the conversa-

> **" BEING THE DUMBEST PERSON ON YOUR TEAM DOESN'T MAKE YOU A STUPID PERSON; IT MEANS YOUR SMART ENOUGH TO SELECT PEOPLE TO WORK WITH THAT YOU CAN LEARN FROM.**

tion based on their area of expertise. We'll be discussing an upcoming shoot and all I'm thinking about is how I can prepare to be the best on set. Suddenly my makeup artist will bring up a few concerns around makeup transitions and I'll just sit there quietly, dumbfounded, because I have no idea what a highlight is. I didn't know people were using highlighters on their face now! Isn't that like ink poisoning or something? Then my agent will start discussing exclusivity around the photos and use a whole bunch of acronyms that I've never heard before. I feel like a mother who is reading her child's Twitter feed and needs to Google the meaning of "LMAO." The point I'm making is that all of these questions and ideas are things I would never think of or, to be honest, don't have the capacity to think of. I'm not a trained makeup artist and I don't know how to be an agent. So what do I do? I own being the dumbest and I ask questions.

What good would it be to surround yourself with smarter people if you can't learn from them? There seems to be this universal fear of "looking stupid" or "sounding dumb." Who is dumber, the person who pretends they know everything, or the person who doesn't and asks questions? Wasting an opportunity to learn seems pretty dumb to me. It's difficult, though, to let go of the idea that people may view you as "stupid." At the end of the day, we all care to some extent what other people think (except maybe Kanye West—he might not care what anyone thinks). But what's more important: doing a good job or saving face?

When I was on the set of my first-ever feature film, *Dr. Cabbie,* I become great friends with Kunal Nayyar, aka Raj from *The Big Bang Theory.* Yes, he talks to girls in real life. Every time he would act a scene out, I was mesmerized by how invested he was in his character. If his character was sad, Kunal felt that pain and it showed on-screen. I also noticed that after a scene, Kunal didn't always feel the need to watch playback. I was obsessed with checking playback because I wanted to make sure I looked okay in the scene. When I asked him about it, he dropped a knowledge bomb that would help me in several areas of my life. He said, "People get too concerned about looking stupid on-screen and so they constantly check the playback. You can't be scared of looking stupid. Instead, just be how your character is supposed to feel." I think that's a great rule to live by when it comes to "looking stupid." Doing a good job should be more important than how you look. With that lesson in mind, I created a rule for myself: if you don't understand something, ask questions until you do understand it. And I mean REALLY understand it. If that takes two or three questions, then so be it. That's not

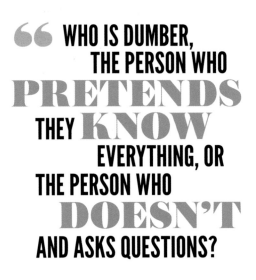

66 WHO IS DUMBER, THE PERSON WHO PRETENDS THEY KNOW EVERYTHING, OR THE PERSON WHO DOESN'T AND ASKS QUESTIONS?

"looking dumb," that's being dedicated to learning something new. I know now that a highlight is something that goes on your cheekbone with powder, not a Sharpie. People have stopped looking at me weird.

I think it's essential for growth to occasionally surround yourself with people who are smarter than you. A big reason I moved from Toronto to L.A. was because when it came to YouTube, I was the most knowledgeable person in my hometown. Before I moved, people would approach me and ask, "You make money off YouTube?" and I would have to explain that ads ran on my videos, so yes, I did. When I moved to L.A., people were suddenly asking me questions about my watch time, pre-roll ads, and how

I window my content. I was like a deer in headlights because I had no idea! All these people were smarter than me when it came to YouTube, and it forced me to become better.

During my Streamy Award acceptance speech, I said something very important that I would like to repeat here. As I stood in front of a roomful of fellow creators, I said, "People always say that if you're the smartest person in the room, then you're in the wrong room. Looking around, I can definitely say that I'm absolutely in the correct room, because you're all so talented and inspirational." At the end of the day, you can't learn new things if you're always the one giving the lessons. You need to be around people who challenge you, intimidate you, and teach you new things. Being a Bawse isn't always about being the best; it's about placing yourself in the best situations.

If I ever feel like I know more about legalities than my lawyer, then I know my lawyer is no longer right for the job. If I ever start managing myself better than my actual manager, then there's a problem. If I'm always in rooms that are overly comfortable, then I'm in the wrong rooms. The only way you can become smarter is by giving yourself a chance to be dumb sometimes.

So go forth and be dumb, but just don't hurt yourself. Don't play with stray Doggs, and if you touch something hot, drop it.

Thanks for the tip, Snoop.

CHAPTER 33

YOU'RE AN INVESTMENT

I HAVE A FRIEND

named Lindsey Stirling who just happens to be, in my opinion, one of the most talented people on the planet. Lindsey is a musician who freezes time with her violin, or at least that's what it feels like. She has millions of views on her YouTube videos, and when I say millions, I'm not talking one or two. One of her videos has 156 million views. One video. The first time I ever saw Lindsey perform was at one of her concerts in Los Angeles with thousands of other audience members. Lindsey is an extraordinary performer who dances, leaps across the stage, and nails quick costume changes, all while keeping her toes pointed AND playing the violin flawlessly. Basically what I'm trying to say is that Lindsey is amazing and super-successful. That's why I was utterly shocked to hear that she still takes violin lessons and—pause for dramatic effect—practices every day. Every. Single. Day.

When Lindsey told me about her lessons, I thought, "Okay, I feel like your teacher is just making FREE money because um, hello, YOU'RE LINDSEY STIRLING." I'm pretty sure that if I Google the words "violin player," a picture of Lindsey will show up. In fact, let me try right now. BRB.

Okay, back. I WAS RIGHT. Her picture came up, no joke. Why on earth is she taking lessons? Lindsey explained to me that there's still so much more she feels she can learn when it comes to her craft. Every day she practices little finger movements that allow her to play a little smoother. She demonstrated one of the movements to me, and I watched in amusement as she held an imaginary violin and moved her pinky exactly one centimeter from left to right.

What I learned from Lindsey that day, and what I continue to learn on my journey to becoming a Bawse, is that you are never too good to stop investing in yourself. We live in a constantly evolving environment, so we need to evolve and grow. Your best today may not be enough next year, so keep developing.

Here are a few ways you can invest in yourself using time, energy, and money:

1 TIME

When I graduated from university and got my degree, I remember thinking that I would never be a student again. Little did I know that I would continue being a student for the rest of my life, because learning never stops. After all, the best teachers in the world are the ones who are still students.

Learning new things means taking the time to read books, watch YouTube videos (hello, self-plug), and attend events that will expand your current knowledge base. For example, when my social campaign #Girl-Love started to get serious momentum, I began taking time out of my day to research women's issues. Through various articles, Emma Watson's speeches (bless her soul), and books, I taught myself new things about gender inequality that I'd previously known nothing about. Investing this time helped shape the future of #GirlLove and made me a better advocate for women's rights.

2 ENERGY

Due to ATP and carbohydrates, everything I'm talking about will, scientifically speaking, require energy. But honestly, don't be that person and correct me. Investing energy into yourself refers to taking classes (like Lindsey), practicing your craft (like Lindsey), and ensuring that you're making decisions that will benefit you (I don't stalk her but this is probably like Lindsey too). These things require not only time but focus and repetition and therefore energy. For example, if you're a vocalist, take singing classes, practice in the shower, and choose not to smoke cigarettes. You're never so good at anything that you can stop putting energy into getting better. Some of the top actors in the industry still have acting coaches, choreographers still take dance classes, and The Rock still has a personal trainer. He could probably personally lift a train, but he still chooses to work with a trainer, which leads me to my next point . . .

3 MONEY

When I first started gaining momentum in the entertainment industry I was hesitant about bringing a manager on board. I was confident that I could handle everything that was being thrown my way and I didn't need to pay someone. It wasn't until my inbox became flooded with thousands of unread emails and I began missing booking opportunities that I decided it was time to hire a manager. Over the years my career has grown at a rapid pace and I am constantly adding people to my team. With every new hire, whether it's a lawyer, assistant, or editor, I am hesitant because, well, no one works for free. I didn't want to keep adding to the list of people I would have to pay. My outgoing payments were starting to add up, and as a business owner (and person of Indian descent), I found myself really concerned. Over time, though, I noticed that the more money I spent, the more money I made. Investing in a team has allowed me to produce more content, make more brand deals, and create more revenue streams. Additionally, investing in a team has given me more time and more opportunities and has generally helped my business to grow. The best example of money well invested is my PR team (probably one of my biggest expenses each month). I was hesitant to spend the money on PR because I thought, "I am my own PR company. I have 10 million subscribers." But again, you're never too good to get better. Since hiring my publicists, I've gotten on *The Tonight Show Starring Jimmy Fallon* and *The Daily Show with Trevor Noah* and have been featured in countless magazines. None of this happened overnight, and I did not make back the money I invested immediately, but the long-term results were worth the money and the wait.

Another way to invest money in yourself is by supporting your own projects. This book is a great example of that. When the conversation started about how to announce this book to my audience, I wanted the idea to be epic. I didn't want to simply tell my audience at the end of one of my videos that I was writing a book, nor did I want to post an Instagram pic with the big news. I wanted to do something above and beyond, and as with most things, above and beyond meant spending money.

As part of my publishing deal, there was no budget for any type of special announcement, and so whatever I decided to do would have to come out of my own pocket. I knew my goal was to create a very special announcement and get the word out, so I invested a decent amount of money into creating a visually stunning short film promoting my book. It was expensive and physically and mentally taxing, but time, energy, and money were the investments required to make it happen. A few weeks later I announced my book on *The Tonight Show* (hello, return-on-investment PR team), and the next day I uploaded my above-and-beyond announcement video. As I write this, I haven't reaped any direct benefits from this investment. I will likely never make back from Ad Sense revenue (the ads playing on the video) what I spent on that video, and that's okay. I made the video to help establish myself as an author, by getting more eyes on my book, and I'm hoping to reap the benefits in the long run.

You are revolutionary. You have amazing ideas. You have the ability to create, to change, to solve, and to influence. Don't sell yourself short by not spending your time, energy, and money on creating the best version of yourself. Instead of buying the new iPhone, which will be slightly bigger, slightly faster, slightly more waterproof, and ten times more expensive, use that money and bet on yourself. Instead of scrolling mindlessly through Facebook and checking in on what everyone else is doing, use that time to check in on what's happening in your life.

I would tell you to also spend your energy on yourself, but your body uses ATP and carbohydrates to create energy that is used for everything you do, so reading this very book is causing you to expend your energy. HA! Got ya, suckaaaaaaa.

No, but for real, invest in yourself.

Make an Investment

Outline one investment in each currency that will help you reach your goals.

Time: _____

_____

Energy: _____

_____

Money: _____

_____

CHAPTER 34

EFF

PROTOCOL

EARLY ON, WE LEARN

that it pays to follow the rules. When I was in elementary school, I got good grades for coloring inside the lines in art class and praise for running basketball drills within the pylons in gym class. Even as an adult I'm expected to drive my car inside a narrow lane on a narrow road while stuck in traffic, surrounded by open land. After going through security at an airport there is a yellow line I can't cross until the customs officer says so. Once I noticed an officer was free and so I stepped ahead on my own. He stopped me, sent me back to the line, waited all of two seconds, and then called me forward. Ah, good old protocol.

In my opinion, some protocol is necessary for the world to function efficiently. Rules and systems need to be in place so that people don't run completely wild. Imagine a world without laws, single-file lines, or etiquette. Sounds like the buffet line at an Indian wedding reception—just thinking about that stresses me out. So what I'll say is this: rules are important MOST of the time. But there are other times when you should eff protocol. Think about it. If everyone followed protocol *all the time,* no one would ever do something for the first time. Nothing would change. No one would stand out—or stand up to injustice.

Take Malala Yousafzai, for example. Malala grew up in Pakistan, where women are denied the right to a high school education. That's the rule. But at a very young age, Malala took a stand, and she's been fighting for female education ever since, despite daily threats to her life. By challenging the system, Malala changed not only her own life but the lives of countless young girls who have been forced to end their education before ever reaching high school. In 2014, Malala was awarded the Nobel Peace Prize. She was seventeen years old.

I'm inspired by Malala's courage every day. I think there are so many lessons to be learned from her story. And while there's no way I can compare any example from my life to the brave actions of a hero like Malala, I recognize that on the most basic level, she broke the rules, and there's

so much value in that. Giving protocol a big middle finger (well, average-sized, in my case—I'm not Godzilla) has proven fruitful in my life more than once. Here's just one example.

As you may know, The Rock is my hero. Always has been. When I was in fourth grade, I jumped for joy when I found out Dwayne Johnson would be doing a signing in my city. On the day of, as soon as the bell rang after school I ran to my uncle's car and we raced to the mall where the event was being held. Once we parked, I speed-walked to the door daydreaming about all the great conversation I was about to have with The Rock. Maybe he would take a liking to me and adopt me! My parents would understand. I mean, it's The Rock! If he wants a child, he should get a child.

I saw a huge line of people and I knew I was headed in the right direction. I glanced at the front of the line in the hopes of catching a glimpse of the star wrestler—and I did. Except it wasn't The Rock, it was Mankind (another wrestler, not all of humanity). What. Was. Happening?! In extreme panic I asked a security guard where The Rock was, and he said that at the last minute WWF (This was before it was the WWE #Always-Remember) had sent Mankind instead of my future father. I was crushed.

That marked the beginning of my lifelong quest to meet the man who inspired me for most of my upbringing. From that day forward, I flew to wrestling events around the world whenever I could, trying to meet him. There was always something standing in my way, though: security measures (makes sense), my ticket not being VIP enough, or simply lacking the funds to purchase a meet-and-greet. I tweeted him again and again, mentioning him in my videos, constantly repeating that meeting him was the number one thing on my bucket list.

Fast-forward to many years later and, through a series of fortunate events, God somehow blessed me enough to receive an email in my inbox from Dwayne. Through my work on YouTube we've become friends, and I vividly remember having a mild panic attack when he actually gave me his number. For a year I would text him every once in a while, still having no clue what it would feel like to meet him in person.

You've already read the story of my experience meeting Dwayne, and so I'll keep this brief. Having said that, I would like to highlight a specific part of the story for the sake of this chapter. In the entertainment industry, protocol is the law, or at least that's what I've been taught. No matter how minor an event is, you schedule it and send a calendar invite. Need to borrow a pen from my desk? How's 4:03 P.M. today for that pen pickup? I'll send an invite. On a red carpet, you dress to meet a certain unspoken dress code, no matter how impossible and uncomfortable it is to walk in those shoes. And talent doesn't speak to other talent to set meetings—your people speak to their people. When it came to The Rock, I followed protocol. As a result, even though I'd become text buddies with Dwayne, I still wasn't any closer to meeting him in person. I got my manager to email everyone and their mothers and still nothing happened. I tried going through my agency to set up a meeting, but every time the result was just a lot of empty promises. I kept trying to navigate the system to check off the number one thing on my bucket list. It never worked.

The night before the MTV Movie Awards, an event I knew Dwayne and I would both be attending, I emailed my entire team (for the millionth time) practically begging them to make a meeting happen. I knew I would be in the audience and he would be backstage and I would not have the credentials to get into his area. After sending the email, I paused for a second, then said, "You know what? Eff this. This system is stupid, and I'm going to do this my way." I pulled out my phone and directly texted Dwayne asking him if I could meet him the next day. Now, this may not seem like a big deal and you might be thinking, "OBVIOUSLY! Why wouldn't you text him?" but in the entertainment industry everyone will convince you that's inappropriate and wrong. In my head I was breaking all the etiquette rules. I took a risk because I wasn't going to let mankind ruin my chance again (this time I'm talking about humanity, not the wrestler). The result? The next day, not only did Dwayne kiss me on the cheek, but he recorded the entire thing on his phone because he'd been looking forward to the meeting too. He made sure I got the credentials I needed to access the greenroom he was in, and it was the most magical moment of my life. Hey, protocol, eff you! You Jabroni!

Since this meeting, there have been countless other times in my career that I've made a request or suggested something outside of the box and the response has been, "This is not how things are traditionally done." Well, here's the thing: a Bawse doesn't need to always do things the way they're traditionally done. A Bawse does things however they need to be done, by any means necessary. I have made a career out of making videos on the Internet that involve me dressing up like my parents and drawing a beard on my face, so don't tell me about all the "traditional" protocols I need to follow. Sometimes I also get told about how my business should be operating and how involved I should be. I've been told that it's not appropriate or necessary for me to be looped in on email threads regarding my own business, because that's protocol. If protocol means I can't see every email that involves decisions being made about ME, then protocol can go directly to jail without passing Go and receiving $200. I don't care about the system people are used to; I care about the system that works for my business.

Whatever you do in life, there will be protocols and rules. The majority of the time, you should probably follow them. But every once in a while, if you feel like a rule is not accommodating to the magic you could create, draw outside of the lines, knock over the pylons, and cross the yellow line. Break the rules and get things done. Sometimes it'll result in something magnificent, and sometimes it might result in complete chaos, but sometimes it's better to ask for forgiveness than to ask for permission.

So break boundaries and go beyond the limits set in place. Don't let a system and the people who exist in it tell you how you should act if it doesn't feel right to you. Do things your way. Break the system!

How's 4:11 P.M. for that system breakage? I'll send an iCal invite.

What? Some rules just make sense.

CHAPTER 35

BE
SANTA

"OH, I DIDN'T

see you there, Bawse," said no one ever. Of course you notice a Bawse. They walk with purpose, speak with confidence, and light up a room, so it's impossible to miss them. In *The Exorcism of Emily Rose,* you thought she turned her head all the way around because she was possessed? Wrong. She just saw a Bawse enter a room.

One of the most identifiable qualities of a Bawse is their energy. Something about them stands out and leaves a lasting impression on people. They are not easily overlooked or forgotten. I learned the power of having presence when I had my first meeting with my current multi-channel network (MCN), Studio 71. For your information, an MCN is essentially like a record label but for YouTube content. My meeting was with the head of the company, Michael, and I knew I had to make a great first impression. We did the "Hi, how are you, nice to meet you" bit, and then he asked me "So, what can I tell you about the company?" Now, as much as I wanted to make a great impression and get signed by this company, I also knew my own value and wanted to make sure the company was right for me. I wanted to be with a company that would work hard for me and vice versa. So, with a smile on my face and a little bit of sass on my tongue, I replied, "You tell me. What can YOU tell ME about the company?" I'll never forget the look on everyone's face when I uttered those words. He looked at me with amusement, and I could tell I'd totally thrown him off guard. Like a Bawse.

After a few minutes of him pitching the company to me (due to my curveball), he finally asked, "What do you want to achieve?" To this I responded with complete honesty. I said, "World domination," with a straight face. After a beat—you know, for dramatic effect—I began to elaborate on everything I wanted to accomplish. There was so much *presence* in the room that the past and future started feeling insecure.

The meeting finished, we shook hands, and I went on with my day. Shortly after, the head of the digital department emailed me to tell me that Michael had said, "She's an absolute star. Let's make sure we get it right." Turns out that Michael was impressed by our meeting and gave his blessing to sign me. Later that week I signed with Studio 71, and we've had a great relationship ever since. I work hard for them and they work hard for me.

First impressions are important, but they aren't the only times you'll need to demonstrate your Bawse presence. Below are guidelines on how to not only make a great first impression but also impress people beyond that first encounter:

1 SMILE FOR A REASON

We've been trained to smile on demand when we meet someone new. It's the polite and expected thing to do. However, a Bawse doesn't just smile because they're supposed to. That wouldn't be genuine. To have true presence, smile for a reason. Smile when you hear someone's name, smile when they tell you what they do, and smile when they tell you how they know your friend. I'm not suggesting that you stare at someone blankly when you first meet them, but don't show off your pearly whites right away. Smile in response to meeting someone new based on something they do or say, not just because it's the conventional thing to do. And give yourself bonus points if you smile while repeating someone's name after you meet them. This gesture acknowledges that you are happy to have met this specific person and you aren't just going through the motions.

2 LISTEN TO UNDERSTAND

We often listen to people talk so that we can respond to what they're saying and NOT because we want to understand what they're saying. Instead of thinking of a response while someone is speaking, pause and focus on what they are actually telling you. Really think about it. Then engage and ask questions to further understand and continue the conversation. Being present means showing interest in what people have to say.

I learned the importance of showing interest from my friend Bridgit Mendler. The first time I met her was during my trip to Kenya in 2016, and I quickly noticed how engaged she was with other people. When I told her about my recent musical project, she didn't change the topic to her projects or music, despite the fact that she's a singer herself. Instead, she listened to me talk about my song and then asked me questions about it: *So, do you plan to release an album? Where can I find it? How much music do you have out?* When I replied, she would think about what I said and then continued to engage me on a deeper level. I left our conversation feeling super-special and remembering every detail of what we talked about. Being a good listener and a great conversationalist is key to having true presence.

DON'T BE ROBOTIC

Just as you've been trained to smile when meeting someone new, you've also been programmed to speak a certain way. When someone asks, "How are you?" you will likely say, "Good. How are you?" But are you really good? Is that truly an accurate reflection of how you're feeling? If you want to have great presence, mean what you say. You'll make much more of an impression if you say, "You know what, I'm actually pretty good. I woke up feeling a bit under the weather but this party has cured me. What about you?" It sounds more interesting and it may even spark conversation. Maybe even tell this person how many times you threw up this morning because you were hungover. Or maybe not.

LIVE IN THE MOMENT

The best way to have presence is to be present (MIND = BLOWN). This means that when you're at an event or talking to someone, be there entirely. Don't constantly check your phone or be thinking about something else. Instead, take in your surroundings, meet new people, be interested in what's going on, and absorb the energy of the room. Not only will you probably have a better time, but you'll appear more approachable. No one wants to approach someone who is scrolling through Instagram stalking their ex.

TIP: Before you enter a room, commit to being present by saying a simple sentence like, "For the next sixty minutes, I am entirely here and nowhere else."

BE CONFIDENT

It's no secret that a big part of having great presence is being confident. Confidence is one of those things that is easy to talk about but is sometimes difficult to have. Don't worry, I got you! Below are a few ways to boost your confidence and let it shine:

DRESS COMFORTABLY Regardless of what everyone else is wearing and what magazines say you should wear, dress in a way that makes you feel awesome. If ripped jeans, sneakers, and a sweatshirt make you feel beautiful and confident, then wear that outfit. Alternatively, if high heels and a miniskirt make you feel wonderful, wear that instead. It's all about how you feel in the clothes you wear. If you're uncomfortable in your clothes, you likely won't be confident, no matter how impressive the brands you're wearing. So try your outfit on, move around, and feel it out. If you're constantly pulling up your pants to hide your butt crack, you should probably change.

It's also important to dress the part. If you're going out for a fun evening, make sure you're dressed in clothes that make you FEEL fun. If you're going to meet new business partners, dress in clothes that make you feel like a ballin' CEO. The clothes don't need to be expensive; they just need to make you feel a certain way. Believe it or not, clothes can evoke certain emotions in us. I know this because I cannot play my parent characters well without dressing up like them. I once read an interview with Jennifer Lawrence in which she too said she couldn't truly get into a character unless she was in costume.

POWER POSES Before you go to an event and/or meet new people, look in the mirror for a few minutes and do some power poses. You should probably be alone for this or things could get weird. Look at yourself and pose like Superman (or Superwoman) with one arm in the air. Make a dramatic, sexy face like you see in movie posters. Raise your chin and give yourself a wink. Fix your collar even if it's completely fine! Why? Because you're powerful and sexy and you do what you want. Looking at yourself in the mirror and seeing yourself the way you want other people to see you is a great way to inspire confidence.

LISTEN TO YOUR JAMS Listen to music that makes you feel confident and powerful. For example, when getting ready to go out I always listen to Rihanna because her music makes me feel awesome and sexy. This may seem like a minor thing, but listening to music that pumps you up will send signals to your brain and set a certain tone. A word of caution: I'd suggest staying away from Adele if you need to be happy and confident. Adele has more of a "getting ready to console a friend whose boyfriend cheated on her"–type vibe.

"

THERE WAS
SO MUCH *PRESENCE*
IN THE ROOM
THAT THE
PAST **AND** FUTURE
STARTED FEELING
INSECURE.

"

SPEAK IN STATEMENTS When you speak to people, make sure you're speaking at an audible volume. Speaking softly will make you seem less confident. Another tip: unless you're actually asking a question, don't sound uncertain. Start strong and end strong. Say things as if everyone really wants to hear them. Just make sure you give everyone else a chance to speak too!

BODY LANGUAGE Body language can often speak louder than words. Crossing your arms or putting your hands in your pockets will make you seem unapproachable. If you aren't directly facing someone while they are talking to you, it will seem like you're not paying full attention. Slouching makes you seem less confident. Walking slowly can make you seem less certain. Whenever you do anything with your body, I want you to feel purposeful and powerful. Stand as if someone is creating a statue of you in that very moment. Walk as if there is an explosion happening behind you and you're an action movie star walking away.

If you're not used to doing any of the above, it may seem like a lot of work. And you know what? At first it is. No one said having presence was easy. If that was the case, everyone would have it. But you're a Bawse and you need to start acting, talking, and walking like one. The next time you walk into a room, just remember one thing: be Santa. Why? Because he always has presents.

CHAPTER 36

SAY
WHAT YOU
MEAN

<----------------->

YOU'RE IN A FIGHT

with your partner and you're texting back and forth. You're sending paragraphs upon paragraphs and you're fuming. You know exactly why you're mad and you think your feelings are completely justified. You receive a reply and start banging away at the keyboard with your own response. Before pressing send, you pause and think, "Wait, is this response okay?" You run your response by your friend just to make sure. *Is this wording okay? What about this emoji? Is it too much or too little?* I used to do this a lot. My camera roll was full of conversation screenshots until I learned one important lesson, and that is: say what you mean. If you say what you mean, you don't need someone to edit your words. Your feelings are authentic to you and therefore don't need revision.

There's great beauty in speaking in straight lines. I currently live in L.A., and in my opinion L.A. is the land of empty words. Don't get me wrong, I love it here. There are palm trees and vegetarian food options for days. But I've found that the social norm is to just say whatever sounds good. I'll have a five-minute conversation with a stranger, and they will end the conversation with "Love you!" I can literally go out for dinner with someone once and they will text me a few days later saying, "Miss ya!" How can you love me if you don't know me? And how can you miss me if you don't know what it's really like to spend time with me? I get that "love you" and "miss you" sound friendly and polite, but what's polite about lying?

The same idea applies when you run into someone you haven't seen in a while and they end the conversation with "Let's grab a coffee soon. I'll text you!" We both know I'm never getting that text, but it sounds polite to say it. However, it's actually not polite because it's not sincere. A Bawse doesn't make empty gestures; a Bawse says what they actually mean. A better response would be "It was really nice seeing you. Hope I run into you again." That sounds just as polite, but it's not filled with fake fluff.

Communication should be relatively easy, but we often make things complicated by not saying what we mean. We convince ourselves that we need to sugarcoat things to such a degree that our actual message ends up buried in sprinkles. Or we beat around the bush and people have to solve a puzzle to understand what we're saying. I believe you can be both charming and straightforward. I was at a party once and across the room from me was an incredibly handsome man. I kept catching myself staring at him and thinking, "OMG, my girlfriends back in Toronto would absolutely die if they saw this beautiful man." Instead of stalking him the whole night or orchestrating a forced conversation with him, I approached him and told him exactly what was on my mind. Well, almost exactly what was on my mind (*meow*). I said, "Hey, my name is Lilly and this is going to sound a little weird, but I have a girls' chat group with my friends back in Toronto and I think they would find great joy in seeing a picture of you. Do you mind taking a picture with me so I can show them how incredibly hot you are? If you don't mind, that is!" He laughed and happily agreed (duh).

I'm also a big believer in the phrase "Say what you mean, but don't say it mean." Being straightforward doesn't mean you have to be rude or harsh. There's always a way to be open and honest while also being respectful. Anyone who behaves otherwise is just being lazy. This mentality is particularly helpful when you need to confront someone. To be honest, I've never been any good when it comes to confrontation, but the more I focus on saying what I actually mean, the easier it gets. In the past, whenever I had issues with any of my employees, I used to rehearse what I would say, making sure to sound professional and stern. It would stress me out and I would usually mess up during the actual conversation. But once I started just saying what I meant, communication became a lot more efficient.

Here's an example of how I changed my communication style:

THE ISSUE: My assistant keeps forgetting to do tasks.

BEFORE: "Hey, I need you to remember to do tasks because forgetting is unacceptable. I asked you to send two emails today and it didn't happen. Please ensure this doesn't happen again."

AFTER: "Hey, it's stressful for me when you forget to do tasks I've asked you to do. Constantly having to remind you defeats the purpose of having an assistant. I'd really like you to figure out a system that allows you to remember things."

The "before" just sounds like office jargon. Literally, Siri could have said it. The "after" represents how I actually feel and exactly why the behavior is problematic for me.

No matter what the situation is, it's always tempting to rehearse dialogue so that you say what you think you're supposed to say. Preparation and gathering your thoughts are awesome, but only if it results in meaningful and genuine communication. Bawses don't just say things; they communicate with purpose. We're so used to communicating at a surface level that we often underestimate the power of communicating on a deeper, more human level. For example, I recently had to bail on one of my friends who had asked me to grab lunch. I forgot about one of my deadlines and texted him the day before to cancel. I was bummed because I hadn't seen him in so long. This could have gone two ways:

SAY WHATEVER:

"Hey, I'm so sorry but I've got to cancel lunch tomorrow. I forgot I had a deadline. Can we reschedule? Thanks!"

SAY WHAT YOU MEAN:

"Hey, I'm so sorry but I've got to cancel lunch tomorrow. I forgot I had a deadline. I was looking forward to seeing you and I'm disappointed I can't now. Please don't think this has anything to do with my desire to hang out with you, and I really hope we can reschedule."

Saying what you mean makes life a lot easier to navigate. People will be impressed that you don't sound like a robot and actually have human emotions. Also, instead of forcing people to read between the lines, you can allow them to read the actual lines, which saves everyone a lot of time and energy. Communication shouldn't be a guessing game. It should be productive and straightforward.

With that said, I don't want to just thank you for buying this book; rather, I want to genuinely tell you how grateful I am. I've worked really hard on writing this with the intent of making you laugh and inspiring you. I don't know everything about success, but I'm confident about what I've written in these fifty chapters. The fact that you're taking valuable time out of your day to read my book, when you could be doing anything else, is really special. Thanks for giving me a chance.

SINCERELY,
NOT SIRI

"

THERE'S ALWAYS A WAY TO BE OPEN **AND HONEST WHILE ALSO BEING** RESPECTFUL. **ANYONE WHO BEHAVES OTHERWISE IS JUST BEING** LAZY.

"

CHAPTER 37

NOT VERYONE HATES YOU

IF THINGS DON'T

constantly go your way, it's probably because the world has weekly meetings discussing how to knock you down. It's true. It's like you're a Plastic and we're all Lindsay Lohan. This is *Mean Girls*. You got cast without auditioning.

Sorry to burst your bubble, but you aren't that special.

Concluding that your failures and shortcomings are caused by other people and situations is a great way to give up all of your power. It's also a great way to take the easy route in life and draw attention away from any real issues that need resolving. In my opinion, when people say things like "Nothing ever works out for me," the real problem is that they're unwilling to change something or try a different tactic. Or when people say "everyone is against me," the real problem is that they aren't willing to see things from a different point of view. In reality, people are too busy worrying about themselves to devise some master plan to destroy you.

When I was a student, my friends would all say the same thing to me: "Lilly, you always need to be right." We all got along so well, but as soon as an argument started, they would drop that line and I would become instantly offended. I didn't NEED to be right. I WAS right. For years I would think that everyone was just jealous of my superior correctness in life. My parents, friends, and fellow dancers were all wrong and I was right . . . um, not that I NEEDED to be, though. It's not my fault I was blessed. I literally felt like I was that one presumably crazy person in a horror movie who hears voices and sees dead people. Everyone else in the movie thinks she's insane and they send her to an asylum. They diagnose her with some mental disorder and then drive back home, only to be killed by seven different ghosts! Turns out she wasn't crazy after all! She was right all along! That was me . . . the absolutely correct victim in the asylum.

Except I was wrong.

As I grew older and began to hear "Lilly, you always need to be right" over and over again, I started to think, "What if that's true? What if EVERYONE else isn't wrong and I'm just too stubborn to take a look at myself and identify my flaws?" It was definitely a lot easier to assume everyone was out to get me. Eventually I made a promise to address my bad habit, and now when I have disagreements with people, I don't view the conversation in terms of right and wrong. Shifting my mentality took a lot of effort and didn't happen overnight. In fact, it took years to create my new mantra, which is, "There is no wrong or right. There's just different." Repeating this to myself has helped me be less hung up on "winning arguments." I only came to this realization because I stopped feeling sorry for myself and started paying attention to the signs the universe was giving me.

Realizing that you have a weakness everyone but you can see is a tough pill to swallow. It's difficult to believe and it's even harder to fix. But a Bawse knows that accepting a weakness is the first step to strengthening that part of you.

If your last three bosses all fired you, maybe it's not because they're jerks. Maybe you don't work hard enough. If your last two boyfriends cheated on you, maybe you're causing them to cheat. Maybe not . . . but maybe you are. I'm not saying a flaw within you validates their behavior, but I'm simply pointing out that it could be a reaction to something you're doing. Maybe you trust too much too fast.

I went through a period when I felt like all my friends were liars. It seemed like every week I would find out someone lied to me about something. After the fourth friend lied to me, I had to step back and take a look at myself. I discovered that my friends were lying to me because they didn't feel they could talk openly with me. Every time they tried I'd create an unwelcoming environment and they feared our friendship would end. Whether or not I believe that fear justifies lying is irrelevant; the fact remains that something within me was causing several people to act in the same way, and thus it made more sense to adjust my behavior. It's about working with what's in your control (see the chapter Play Nintendo).

At the end of the day, we're all reactive beings. We react to the environment we're in. So if several people are reacting negatively to you in the same exact way, maybe it's because you're doing something to cause that reaction. If that's the case, you have two options: (1) get a tattoo across your chest of Drake's lyrics "I got enemies, got a lot of enemies," or (2) take the hint and work on improving yourself.

Your nipples would get in the way of a tattoo that big anyway.

CHAPTER 38

NDERSTAND

PRIORITIES

ON THE SURFACE,

relationships seem to fail for so many reasons. It's easy to speculate endlessly. Is it because your girlfriend hates it when you go out with the boys to watch sports? Could it be because your boyfriend always skips class to flirt with other girls? Maybe your best friend travels too much and now you feel like you barely know her. We can blame the conflict on the fact that people are inconsiderate, disloyal, selfish, and weird—but once we dig our shovel further into the problems, it's clear that the majority of failed relationships are caused by one thing: having different priorities.

Have you ever been in a fight with a partner or friend and thought, "Wow, how can you not understand that you're wrong?!" I'll just assume you're putting your hands up right now and saying, "Preach!" That's because we have a specific set of priorities that we understand and value, and it's difficult to deal with someone who isn't on the same page. What we need to remember is that priorities are like opinions, because everyone has different ones. AND, most importantly, priorities are not facts. Let me say it again so the people in the back can hear: *priorities are not facts.* This means that they cannot be right or wrong; they're simply different. Wuddup previous chapter reference!

This lesson has been one of the hardest for me to learn in life. Once I learned it, though, it was like a light came on. Everyone has a different "aha!" moment, but let me share mine. While I was on tour in Boston for *A Trip to Unicorn Island,* preparing for my next show, I received word that the next day would be a little nerve-racking, for two reasons. First, we would be shooting the entire stage performance for my documentary, meaning the show had to be flawless. The documentary shoot was stressful because we had only one shot at capturing the footage. The entire crew was flying in with all their equipment, and the associated costs simply wouldn't allow for another chance at another performance in another city. As if this situation wasn't high-stakes enough, Dwayne Johnson's family was coming to see me perform. For obvious reasons, their attendance was both exciting to me and extremely intimidating. I, of course, wanted to make THE BEST impression on his family, especially his daughter, who introduced him to my videos in the first place. Needless to say, the night before, I was an absolute tense mess.

I sat down with my entire cast and crew and thoroughly explained the importance of the next day's show. I emphasized that we needed maximum sleep so we could have maximum energy and perform our best. Stressed, shaking, and stuttering, I kept repeating just how much the show meant to me, like a broken record. (Dear Millennials: A record is an ancient musical medium—like a physical version of a download.) Finally I called everyone in for a team huddle and ended the meeting for the night, since it was almost midnight. As I walked to my hotel room, I turned back briefly and saw, to my complete surprise, that a few of my dancers, two of whom were my oldest, closest friends, were not headed in the same direction. I could hear them discussing going out for a few drinks and food. Absolutely astonished, I walked up to them and exclaimed, "How are you going out right now after everything I just said?!" They responded that they didn't think it was a big deal and they wanted to hang out for a bit. I was so furious, I just walked away. I didn't know what to say. Back in my hotel room, I replayed the incident in my head to see if I'd overreacted. I felt extremely disrespected. I couldn't believe that my two friends, who were also my dancers, could betray me and disregard my feelings during such a stressful time. They were wrong, and nothing would convince me otherwise!

The next day we did the show and it went brilliantly. Everyone performed well, Dwayne's family loved the whole experience, and the crew captured amazing footage. To an outside observer, things would appear to be swell. But on the inside I was still fuming. My friends had contributed to one of the most stressful nights of the tour for me. This fury lasted a few days until I finally just needed to talk to someone. I approached our tour manager, Dave, whom we had all taken to calling "Dad" because, truthfully, that's what he became to us. Dad always took care of us on the road and did everything to ensure we felt our best on- and offstage. With my spirits low, I sat down beside him and said, "I don't get why my friends would do that to me before the most important show. They're so selfish." His reply was blunt but necessary. With kindness in his eyes, he replied, "Lilly, just because something is important to you, it doesn't mean it's important to them."

Have you ever heard something so simple yet profound that it literally felt like a switch had been flipped within you? That's what this felt like. Dad was absolutely right. All of my dancers, my friends included, performed so well every single night. They always put on a great show and never did anything offstage that negatively impacted their presence onstage. If my dancers had gone out that night and then danced horribly the next day, I would have had the right to get upset. But they hadn't. The real reason I was upset was that I had mistakenly thought their personal priorities were identical to mine—a misguided assumption. Dwayne is my childhood hero, not theirs. The footage was for my documentary, not theirs. I was feeling stressed and anxious, and they weren't. They were paid to do a job and they did it remarkably well. They were not being paid to care about what I cared about. Remember when I said nothing would convince me they weren't wrong? Well, Dad found a way.

The same goes for professional relationships. If you start a business with a partner and your personal goals are to do a lot of charity and social work, you may run into issues if your co-worker just wants to make a lot of money. Does wanting to make it big make him wrong? No. Some people want to be rich. Others want to make a social impact. Maybe both of your priorities will change and completely switch later in life, but for the moment they're different.

Now, that doesn't mean that you cannot ever be in a successful relationship with someone with different priorities. You can have the same goals even, but you need to learn to understand each other's priorities and keep them in mind. If you can be mindful of the fact that other people are motivated by their own priorities, you won't feel like they're intentionally disrespecting you. Your boyfriend going out to watch sports instead of hanging out with you for a night doesn't necessarily mean he's selfish. It means that he likes sports and that watching the game is a priority for him. If you absolutely cannot accept someone else's priorities, that's a good indication that maybe you're not the best fit for each other. After all, sometimes we base our expectations of people based on what we want them to prioritize. As with all expectations, you risk disappointment. But if you can learn to work with people in a way that doesn't make them feel like they have to sacrifice everything they care about, you'll go a long way.

A Bawse knows how wonderful it feels when someone respects your priorities. I'll never forget the first time my mom placed importance on my content creation, after I'd spent years trying to get my parents to take my career seriously. My dad was asking me to go somewhere with him, and before I could reply, she told him, "She can't today. It's Thursday and she has to make a video." I beamed with pride. It felt AMAZING to have my priority not only recognized but accommodated, even if in a minor way, by someone I love.

We all have a carrot dangling above our heads. For some people that carrot is money. For others it's family. And still for others it's Instagram likes. The best relationships are those that not only allow you to have your own unique carrot but also allow you to help your partner reach their carrot. If two people get to care about their priorities in addition to caring about each other, that's a win. So don't just assume everyone cares about what you care about. And, more importantly, don't label that space between your priorities as wrong or right. There are 7 billion people on the planet and we're all going to have different carrots.

Bugs Bunny would have a field day—maybe don't go into business with him.

Let's Prioritize

What are your top three priorities in life? (BE HONEST NOW, and remember there are no rights or wrongs.)

1. _____

2. _____

3. _____

What are your boyfriend/girlfriend/mother/father/sister's top priorities?

1. _____

2. _____

3. _____

CHAPTER 39

BE
UNAPOLOGETICALLY
YOURSEL

EVERYONE IS WEIRD.

No matter how "normal" someone seems, I can assure you that they also do very weird stuff. When I make a speech, I wear high heels, a power suit, and eye shadow. I stand up straight and use words like "fathom" and "whom." I look put together, poised, and normal as eff. Then I get backstage to my dressing room, put on my unicorn slippers, tie my hair like a horn on the front of my forehead, and gallop around while making pig noises. If someone asks me what I'm doing, I will respond only in the tone of a dramatic opera singer. That's the weirdo I am, and I'm proud of it.

But there's more to being yourself than being weird.

In this day and age, everyone *thinks* they are being their true selves because they use an abundance of Tumblr quotes indicating so and post double-chin selfies. And I'm here to tell you that a silly selfie with two filters in a cute outfit with a caption that reads "Sorry, not sorry" is a very basic level of "being yourself." I've recently learned that true authenticity is like a beautiful lasagna with many layers. Once you get past the cute cheesy stuff, it gets heavy. I used to live my life thinking I was completely myself. I embraced my weirdness, never pretended to be someone I wasn't, and stood up for what I believed in. If you'd told me that I could be MORE myself, I would have sneered at you: "Are you kidding? I'm SO me. If someone was taking attendance right now and called my name, I would raise both of my hands."

But then I met someone and within an hour she changed everything I thought I knew about being authentic. I was introduced to a new level of realness, an unapologetic type, and it changed my life.

It's October 2015, and I'm holding a jar of pickles and some flaming hot Cheetos (as one should) as I nervously pace back and forth waiting to shoot a video. I'm anxious, excited, and terrified all at the same time. I'm a twenty-seven-year-old child. I approach my manager and start spitting out some inspirational sentences, mostly to reassure myself: "This is going to be totally awesome. I'm just going to be cool. Look how chill I am. I look like the snowflake emoji just ate a chill pill in the Arctic. Mother-effing McFlurry vibes. Brrrrrrr . . ." And then from the back of the room I hear a voice excitedly ask, "Where's Lilly?!"

All chill has left the building. Welcome to the Sahara Desert.

Selena Gomez walks up to me with open arms and gives me a huge hug. EVERYTHING IS FINE. LOOK HOW CHILL I AM. JK. My body could literally be used as the set for *Mad Max*. We sit down, and for the next hour Selena unintentionally schools me on authenticity. The first thing I notice is that Selena has already opened the Cheetos I gifted her and is happily enjoying them while slouched in her seat. She didn't care that her makeup JUST got done. She wanted the Cheetos and so she ate the Cheetos. Then there's me, trying to sit up straight, smile perfectly, and showcase the shirt I bought just for this occasion. *What? This old thing?*

We start talking about her new album, *Revival,* and I make a creepy joke about her album cover: "Girl, look at you! All naked and hot on the cover. I see you." I'm expecting her response to be a giggle or smile along-side an obligatory "thanks," but instead she calmly says, "It's so raw and beautiful." I can't remember a time when someone spoke to me with that level of self-awareness and confidence. She truly believed the cover was beautiful, and so she said it. I think many of us don't own our own beauty because we fear sounding arrogant. But not Sel. She knows that calling yourself beautiful can be empowering, not necessarily cocky.

During the shoot, I make a joke about people thinking my hair is fake. Selena puts her fingers through my hair and says, "You have beautiful real hair. Mine, however, is very fake." No effs given. After the shoot, we take some selfies and I make it a point to show them to Selena for approval. "Hey, Sel, are these okay?" *Also, can we be friends forever, by any chance?* Without hesitation (or even a second look), she responds, "Oh yeah, girl, they're fine." Selena is okay with however she looks in the picture because that's how she looked at that moment.

Now, you might be thinking that I'm completely biased because I'm a huge Selena Gomez supporter. And yeah, you're right. She's amazeballs. But I've had the pleasure of witnessing this unapologetic authenticity of hers time and time again. So let's fast-forward to the second time I met her, at We Day (awesome event aimed at inspiring students) in California. It's a brief meeting, but I'm still a little nervous, and this time I don't have any Cheetos as a peace offering. As soon as I see her I say, "Hey, I don't know if you remember me, but—" and Sel cuts me off. I'm expecting her to say, "Yes, I do, nice to see you again" or "Sorry, remind me of your name again, please." I mean, that's what I've been hearing all day. But once again I'm caught off guard as Selena laughs and lovingly says, "OMG, shut up, you idiot, of course I remember you" as she pulls me in for a hug. In a day filled with protocol and cookie-cutter networking lingo, Selena's refreshing tone and vibe cut through the BS. She doesn't care about sounding any type of way. She speaks how she feels.

Now let's move to the third time I met her (welcome to my book: *The Chronicles of Fangirling over Selena Gomez, Special Edition*), backstage at her concert in Toronto. By this time in my life, I'm a little more collected and don't completely freak out. As soon as I enter the room Selena says, "Argh, I'm so bloated, if you know what I mean." These are her first words. I love this girl. Then we start talking about her tour, and it's at this moment that I officially declare Selena the most unapologetically real person I've ever met. We're talking about ticket sales and she says, "It's been about 70 percent sold out at shows, which is a bit less than last time." Now, I've been on tour before. Granted, my tour wasn't comparable in size to Selena's (I'm not an ex-wizard), BUT if you ever asked me about ticket sales, my deep, hidden insecurities would never allow me to openly say, "It was 70 percent sold out." I'd always felt that I had something to prove. *If my show didn't sell out, then there must be a reason! The venue! The ticket agents! The marketing! Someone, somewhere is racist!* And here is Sel, an A-lister, a pop star, not giving a fraction of an eff about what people think of her ticket sales, telling it like it is. She is so accepting of every part of herself, whether it be her weaknesses, flaws, strengths, or accomplishments. If she feels beautiful, she embraces that feeling and admires herself. If she feels insecure about something, she doesn't shy away but says it openly, without hesitation.

I've changed in the years since I've gotten to know her. I understand the difference between being yourself and being unapologetically yourself on a deeper level. Beyond the weird quirks and self-deprecating jokes I make in interviews, I'm learning to accept all facets of myself. If I'm upset and make a poor decision, I try not to be ashamed. I made that decision. My unique personality and life circumstances helped make that decision, and even if I have to fix whatever mess I caused, I own that decision. If I feel jealous or insecure, I embrace that side of me and proudly communicate it. That's my insecurity and jealousy, and it's who I am in that moment.

With my newfound confidence to be undeniably myself, I decided to make a video called "The Most Honest Q&A Ever" for my YouTube channel. I'd like to direct your attention to two parts of this video:

1. **WHAT WOULD YOU DO IF YOU HAD A MILLION DOLLARS?**

   OLD ANSWER: I'm not really sure. Donate some? Travel? I like to spend money on experiences.

   What I'm Thinking: I want to come across as if money doesn't really matter because people will think I'm materialistic.

   NEW ANSWER: Well, I do have a million dollars, and to be honest, it hasn't changed any major things I do. Money is the result of what I do, not the reason I do it.

   What I'm Thinking: I'm proud that I've worked hard and earned money. I don't need to lie about it. I'm more proud that it hasn't changed me much, though.

2. **ARE YOU A VIRGIN?**

   OLD ANSWER: I think it's so interesting and strange that people ask this.

   What I'm Thinking: Let me curve this answer and avoid giving any real information because I'm embarrassed.

   NEW ANSWER: Yeah, I am. I used to be ashamed to admit that, but honestly, it's my decision.

   What I'm Thinking: I'm proud of my decision, not because I think it's right but because it's mine. My body. My life. My decision. There's no shame in my game.

Answering those questions the way I did filled me with an entirely new and unique feeling of happiness. It's a beautiful thing to have complete self-acceptance. Nothing to prove, nothing to hide. You are who you are, and you should be damn proud, like a BAWSE.

Now if you'll excuse me, someone just called for an über-unicorn (oink, oink) and it's my time to shine. Hopefully it was Sel. I'm craving Cheetos.

CHAPTER 40

SHAKE

WHAT YOUR

MAMA
GAVE YA

<------------------------->

THE FIRST TIME

I ever met Dwayne "The Rock" Johnson, I noticed something very specific about him. You might think I noticed how his right arm could pass as Godzilla's stunt double, or that he's so handsome that I wanted to legally change my name to Scissors just so he might smash me. Yes, I went there. And I'll go there again!

Surprisingly, however, what I remember most vividly about meeting Dwayne wasn't his looks or giant muscles, although, I mean . . . those features are also great. What stood out to me was his behavior around people he just met—in this case, my film crew. He shakes every person's hand when he meets them. And when I say everyone, I mean *everyone*—from my sound guy to my producer, my assistant, and the security guard who is trying to pry me off Dwayne's leg. Which, by the way, stop that and LET ME LIVE. Rock climbing has always been on my bucket list!

I'm going to keep going there.

For someone as rich and famous as Dwayne Johnson, I was shocked that he made a point to introduce himself to every new person he met, even if they didn't initiate the interaction. He acted as if people didn't know exactly who he was, which was both refreshing and impressive. Not only did my entire crew comment on his behavior after we were done shooting, but my friend and fellow YouTube creator Grace Helbig also pointed out this specific trait of Dwayne's after she met him for a shoot. If two girls get together to discuss Dwayne Johnson and, of all things, end up talking about how he shakes people's hands, something is very wrong. Or, perhaps, very right.

Since meeting Dwayne, I've met two other spectacular individuals who behave in a similar fashion. The king of soca music, Machel Montano, walked into my dress rehearsal when I was performing in Trinidad and Tobago. The first thing he did was walk around the entire stadium and shake hands with all my dancers, my stage manager, the AV crew, and even some random people I didn't know who had probably snuck in. After rehearsal, all my dancers commented on how wonderful Machel was. They met many new people that evening, but it was Machel who blew them away. (By the way, if you don't know what soca music is, you need to YouTube-search some Machel Montano right now. Your booty can thank me later.)

The other person whose impeccable manners and class have made a major impact on me is the star of *The Tonight Show,* Jimmy Fallon. He walked into my NYC dressing room the day I was scheduled to be on his show, and we instantly started chatting away about the show and my You-Tube videos until he looked around and abruptly stopped. "Hi, how are you? I'm Jimmy!" he said as he shook hands with my hair and makeup stylists. Hit by a wave of admiration, I thought, "Of course you're Jimmy! This is your show! You're a superstar!" But superstardom didn't stop Jimmy from shaking every person's hand.

Now, you can call it a coincidence, but three of the most successful people I've ever met have all had this distinctive tendency. Not only do they introduce themselves, but they extend a hand to new people because they understand that a good handshake can say a lot about who you are.

After taking note of this, I tried it out for myself. I was in Anaheim, California, for VidCon, which, if you're not familiar with it, is a convention that brings together YouTube creators and fans in the most Armageddon-type way. YouTube creators literally have to swim through a sea of screaming fans to get from panel to panel, and it's exciting and borderline terrifying all at the same time.

After finally making it from my hotel room to the convention center, I was a little drained and not my usual high-energy self. But it was time to shoot "YouTubers Read Mean Tweets" for Jimmy Kimmel's show, and being tired wasn't an option. I walked into the room with a huge smile on my face, and the segment director instantly approached me, introduced himself, and directed me to take a seat in front of the camera. This guy probably had to do a hundred more of these segments, and I could tell he was sticking to a routine. But I had a different plan. Before sitting down, I went around the room and introduced myself to the writer, the assistant, the sound technician, the cameraman, and the security guard. I was shaking what my mama gave me—and that's my hand. I got more stares and shocked looks in that moment than all the other times I've shaken *other* things my mama gave me. I'm serious. What? I like to have fun.

After recording the segment, I thanked everyone and started heading toward the door, only to be stopped by the director. He gave me a smile and said, "Hey, you're really cool. Do you want to check out the show sometime? What's your email?" Fast-forward to three months later, and I'm sitting in the greenroom at a Jimmy Kimmel taping, eating delicious cake and mingling with some pretty rad people. And at that moment I knew: if a behavior results in free cake, one must always perform that behavior.

Since then, introducing myself to everyone in a room has become my mantra. Of course, I do this within reason. I don't walk into a Forever 21 and shake hands with all the customers, because who has any free hands when shopping? And Forever 21 is usually three floors and I simply do not believe in that much cardio. But whenever I walk onto a set or into a meeting, I make it a point to introduce myself, and every single time I do it, I see a flicker of appreciation in people's eyes.

The way I see it, it's on you to create great opportunities. Whenever you meet someone for the first time, you have the opportunity to make a killer first impression and ensure they remember you. So you have two options. You can walk into a room and blend in with the crowd. I mean, this is cool too, you know, if you want to be all those other characters in a *Where's Waldo?* book that people skim over. Or before you enter a room, you can take a deep breath and commit to making a great impression. Yes, it takes a lot of energy and time to make people feel important and valued. And to that I respond, "Boo-effing-hoo." You're a Bawse now, and you need to spend less energy stalking your ex on Instagram and more energy making phenomenal first impressions. Plus, there are so many famous puppies on Instagram now who are way cuter than your ex. Get your priorities straight.

"**YOU'RE A BAWSE** NOW, AND YOU **NEED** TO **SPEND** LESS ENERGY **STALKING** YOUR EX ON INSTAGRAM AND **MORE ENERGY** MAKING **PHENOMENAL** FIRST IMPRESSIONS."

CHAPTER 41

YOUR EX WASN'T RIGHT FOR YOU

IF YOU SKIPPED

straight to this chapter, I'm sorry about your recent breakup. Read this chapter, and then when you're ready and have finished eating your ice cream, you should read the rest of the book too. But now that you're here, welcome to what is probably the most specific chapter of this book. The title implies that your ex, specifically YOUR ex (if you have one; if not, then la dee da), wasn't right for you. That's pretty ignorant of me to conclude since I don't personally know you or your ex (unless I'm your ex, in which case, awkkkwarddddd, because I'm awesome). I don't know why you broke up or whose fault it was, if anyone's. But I do know that if someone is no longer in your life by choice, then they are not right for you. Allow this chapter to be pizza for your heartbreak. Toppings include extra cheese, mushrooms, and a whole lot of truth.

Human beings do this silly thing where they get into relationships. Not all species do that. A lot of species understand the importance of procreating, and so they pee in certain areas, meet up, get jiggy with it, pop some kids out, and move on in life. Maybe they howl at each other every once in a while. But most humans form relationships and are heavily impacted by them. For simplicity's sake, I'm going to split people who experience breakups into two categories:

> **" YOU SHOULD BE SAD ABOUT MISSING SOMEONE AND BEING HURT, BUT YOU SHOULD NOT BE SAD BECAUSE YOU BELIVE THAT PERSON WAS RIGHT FOR YOU. I'M 99 PERCENT CERTAIN THEY WERE NOT.**

the people who get over things relatively quickly and move on with life, and the people who are glued to their bed for three months, wearing clothes covered in BBQ sauce stains. This chapter is for group number two, because for them the chances are that a breakup results in them being unproductive, unmotivated, and the opposite of what a Bawse should be. Why? They are devastated, miss their ex-partner, and are confused by how they can ever fill the hole this person left in their heart. Let's talk about that.

It's necessary to feel your emotions. So if you're devastated due to a breakup, by all means cry it out, stay in bed, and scream at his or her picture. We all know that time heals wounds, so I'm not going to convince you not to mourn. What I want to convince you of is that you should be sad about missing someone and being hurt, but you should not be sad because you believe that person was right for you. I'm 99 percent certain they were not. And if you're in that remaining 1 percent, then just play along anyway. In fact, I might change your mind too. I'm feeling myself!

This entire chapter was created as the result of a conversation I had with one of my friends. I was consoling him about his last breakup, which happened quite a while ago, but he was still affected by it. For the sake of time and everyone's sanity, allow me to summarize the conversation for you. There's no need for trees to die because of this hot mess of a relationship. Let's call my friend Bob and his boyfriend Steve. Yes, welcome to 2017, where love wins.

- Bob and Steve meet. They fall in love.
- Bob and Steve move in together.
- Bob and Steve also work together.
- Bob and Steve spend almost all their time together.
- Bob is very reliant on Steve and has a hard time without him.
- Bob feels confident because of Steve.
- Bob loves Steve more than anything in the world.

Very intense story arc, as you can see. After I finished listening to how much Bob missed having a relationship with Steve, I said, "That sounds like a pretty horrible and unhealthy relationship." Bob was completely taken aback and was confused by what I meant. I know it's difficult to think that a relationship that defined you, made you feel comfortable, and represented love to you isn't actually what love should be. When people tell me about their relationships, they often describe something they believed was "right," but what if that relationship was wrong all along? After all, Bob's and Steve's initials spell BS (zing!). Yeah, your ex was great and it was a wonderful time in your life, but was this person right for you? When you meet someone new and continuously compare them to your ex, are you comparing them to someone who was good for you, or to someone who simply was familiar and represents what you think love is supposed to look like? Is that a fair comparison?

After the conversation I had with my friend, I turned the magnifying glass on myself and analyzed some of my relationships that have ended. I haven't been in too many romantic relationships that have scarred me (I'm definitely person number one), but I've had a lot of friendships that have made a strong impact on me. When I was in college I had a best friend, as most people do, and we were inseparable. Again, for the sake of trees, allow me to summarize:

- Lilly meets friend. They become best friends.
- Lilly tells her friend everything and vice versa.
- Lilly and her friend do everything together.
- Lilly doesn't need to make any new friends because she has her best friend.
- If Lilly's best friend wasn't going to a party, Lilly didn't feel like going.
- Lilly would believe everything her friend told her and vice versa.
- At social gatherings, Lilly would only hang out with her best friend.
- Lilly prioritized her best friend over everyone else.

Lilly sounds lame as eff. Thank God I'm not her. Our friendship ended over a massive argument, and I would constantly tell myself that I'd never have another friend like that friend. I used to live my life thinking there was this void because THAT best friend wasn't there. After my conversation with Bob I had a thought: What if that's not how best friends are supposed to be? I know that seems obvious to you, but the thought never once occurred to me, just like it didn't occur to Bob. What if I'm simply feeling the void of not having that unhealthy relationship? Why would I want a friendship that blinds me to the possibility of making new friends? Why would I not want to go to parties and be independent? Why would I want to be in a friendship that made me ignore other people?

In most cases, when we miss someone who hurt us, it isn't really because they were right for us; it's that they were familiar to us and represented a certain ideal. It's our attachment to an idealized relationship that is hard to let go of. If your friend lied to you, if your lover cheated on you, or if someone simply decided they didn't want to be in a relationship with you anymore, they are not right for you. It may feel like they are, even though they hurt you, but they aren't. You know who is right for you? The person who is everything you love about your ex, except for the part that hurt you. There are 7 billion people on the planet, and it's naive and scientifically ridiculous to believe that such a person does not exist.

So don't trip. Your ex can hold a special place in your heart, a small section called "Memories LOL." You can miss that person,

> **" YOU KNOW WHO IS RIGHT FOR YOU? THE PERSON WHO IS EVERYTHING YOU LOVE ABOUT YOUR EX, EXCEPT FOR THE PART THAT HURT YOU.**

but don't let them define what a relationship is supposed to be. Don't convince yourself that your ex is the only one for you. You experienced one type of love with them, but there are billions of other types just waiting to one-up your experience.

Now, put the darts away and start from the beginning of the book.

OUT OF THE BLUE

2009

When something is broken, you fix it. You use tape, glue, and a few nails. But what if every time you try fixing something, it breaks into smaller pieces, eventually turning into ashes? That's my life right now. I can't fix it. I don't know how, and to be honest, I don't want to. I don't want any part of my life tomorrow to contain the pieces of today or yesterday. I give up on this life and I want a new one.

I'm too cowardly to kill myself, and so I'm going to do the next best thing: move far away. I want to move so far away that I forget about this life. And I want people to forget about me. I have a life worth forgetting. In six months I'm going to move to India and start over.

I already called my aunt, who has an unoccupied house in Punjab. I was vague with my questions, but I got the information I needed. I'm not sure what I'll do there or how I'll survive, but I'll take my chances and hope for the best. That's more than I can hope for here.

I sit in the living room and take a deep breath as my family stares back at me. They have no idea what I'm about to say and they're definitely not going to understand or like it, but I'm ready to shut them out. I'm good at shutting things out. I feel like that's my only talent these days. I tell them my plan and watch as my mother cries. I know she is crying because she hears the unwavering commitment in my voice. She knows this side of Lilly, the side that is stubborn and stuck in her ways. She argues with me and I sit there numb, indifferent to the negativity surrounding me. Her reassurance, comfort, and love aren't strong enough to reach me.

I go to bed with a countdown in my mind: six months to save enough money and get out of this nightmare. I look around my room and already feel disconnected to this world. My decision is to give up. The tiny spark I have left in me goes out. Welcome to the land of no dreams.

2015 Today I decided that I'm done with this life, this comfort zone, and these nerves. I need to move on. I've been cowardly and it's held me back from truly blossoming in my career. I want to move away, and in six months I will. I am finally going to fulfill my dream of moving to L.A.

For months I've been saying I'll do it. My career is going so well, and I know this move will take me even further. I know exactly what I'm going to do when I get there, and that's conquer. I'm going to create an even better life for myself, a life that not only makes me proud but makes my parents proud too.

I sit at my going-away party surrounded by people who love me. My friends and family have all shown up, and I know they will never forget me. I'm going to visit them often, and they'll do the same, I just know it. I show them pictures of my new apartment, the first one I'll ever live in alone, and they beam with pride.

That night, after my friends help me pack, I lie in bed and take a look around my room. I will never feel disconnected from this place, and this will always be home. I cry bittersweet tears as I say goodbye to my comfort zone. I'm not running away from this place, but I am graduating from it.

I've checked my bags and I'm waiting in the security line at the airport. My friends and family are waiting on the other side of the rope to say goodbye and watch me disappear through the gate. I take a deep breath and watch as my mother cries. She's crying because she knows this side of Lilly, the side that is determined and will persevere. She hugs me and I hug her back, feeling her love and support shield me against any negativity. I'm going to make her so proud. I say my goodbyes and disappear through the gate to start the next exciting chapter of my life.

I arrive in my new apartment, nervous and excited. I've been saving up for this and I really did it. I look around and see a life full of opportunity, a life I'm going to make worth remembering. My decision is to conquer this city. I'm finally doing it. The giant spark I have in me doubles in size. Welcome to the land of dreams.

PART 4
BE A
UNICORN

It's time for you to burp a rainbow and poop some Skittles. In this section you will learn about the power of having strong values, the reason to express gratitude, and how to not just coexist with others but positively impact them. You'll also learn how to navigate sticky situations that tempt you to behave poorly. A Bawse knows that the power of compassion, love, and kindness should never be underestimated.

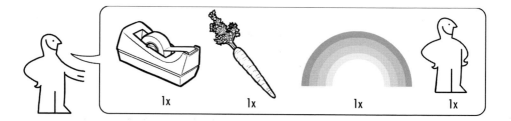

1x   1x   1x   1x

CHAPTER 42

YOU
ARE A
CHAMELEON

YOU SHOULD BE SCREAMING

with rage and disagreeing with me right now. I just called you a chameleon. You. A Bawse. A chameleon? How dare I? And you're right. You should challenge me to a duel. I'm trying to teach you how to stand out from the crowd, make a statement, and be bold, so how dare I call you a chameleon, something that blends into its surroundings? Well, the reality of the situation is that your surroundings influence how you feel, how you think, and how you behave. Have you ever felt optimistic in a room full of pessimists? Have you ever gotten a lot of work done in a room full of people slacking off? Have you ever seen a Happy Meal in a sad place? Probably not. You're a human being and you're a product of your environment. So what does that mean? That means you better create an environment where Bawses thrive.

Right now I'm being super-productive, writing my book, and feeling happy. Why? Partially because I'm a unicorn, but also because I've created a work environment for myself that encourages positivity and creative thinking. On my computer screen there is a sticky note that says "Focus on what deserves your attention." Below that is a desk plate that says "Get it, girl." Amongst my array of colorful, bright office supplies (I have a bright blue stapler that is so fine it could qualify as a Man Crush Monday) is a candle labeled "positive energy." And if I ever make a mistake while writing with one of my lime-green pencils, it's okay because my pink eraser says "Work happy." It looks like Willy Wonka's chocolate factory threw up all over my desk, and I absolutely love it. This workspace makes me feel inspired and encourages me to work my hardest, while also putting a smile on my face.

Creating a physical environment that makes you feel motivated is something that is completely in your control. Whether it's the artwork in your room, your desktop wallpaper, or the color of the Post-its on your desk, your surroundings make a difference, whether you consciously recognize it or not. I'm personally obsessed with colors because they make me feel warm and fuzzy inside. I have seven towels in my apartment, all bright and different colors. My linen closet looks like a Skittles factory.

Every time I put one towel in the wash, I choose a new color, and to be honest, this decision excites me every time. Now, you might be thinking, "What a psycho," and that's what the friend who was staying with me also thought. But whenever I switch my towel, I step out of the shower, I lock eyes with this beautiful new color, and my brain registers the change. In some minor way, I believe it makes my day better. In fact, one evening my house guest approached me and quietly said, "The towels make a difference," and then avoided eye contact as he walked away. OF COURSE THEY DO! Who doesn't want magical rainbow towels? I'd like to believe that even on the days I'm in a rush and can't admire my beautiful towel, my brain still notices it and smiles a little.

OMG. Did I just write an entire paragraph about towels? MOM, GET OUT OF MY HEAD!

FIVE WAYS to Create a Bawse Environment

1. CHOOSE A FACEBOOK, Twitter, and/or email password that is an affirmation or important reminder. Think about it—you write this password several times a day, so you might as well make it meaningful! Even when you're in a rush, you're giving your brain a subliminal message. Some examples: Workhardtoday or Staydetermined or Youdontneedaboyfriendbecauseyourecompletelyfinebyyourselfandifyoueverdoubtthatthenlistentosingleladies (okay, that last one might surpass the character limit).

2. IF YOU STRUGGLE with a certain thought or bad habit, write yourself notes and post them in places where you will constantly see them. My "Focus on what deserves your attention" sticky is meant to remind me NOT to reply to negative YouTube comments and thus is located on the screen of my iMac. If you're not a morning person, put a note on your bathroom mirror that says "The morning is almost over! You're going to have the best day." If you often procrastinate by scrolling through Twitter, make your phone wallpaper something that says "Shouldn't you be working right now?"

66

YOU'RE A HUMAN BEING **AND YOU'RE A PRODUCT OF YOUR** ENVIRONMENT. **SO WHAT DOES THAT** MEAN? **THAT MEANS YOU BETTER CREATE AN** ENVIRONMENT **WHERE BAWSES THRIVE.**

99

3   **CHANGE YOUR RINGTONE** and/or text tone to a song that makes you feel happy. It's important to be as nerdy as possible here. For example, my text tone is Rue's whistle from *The Hunger Games.* Yup, that's right. You can go ahead and idolize me now.

4   **FOLLOW CUTE PUPPIES** on Instagram! Here are some good ones: @jiffpom, @beanzhart, and @marniethedog. And if for some reason you're not fond of cute puppies (which, btw, is super weird and you should probably get checked out), then follow accounts of other things that make you happy, such as kittens, food, or babies. (Or may I suggest @iisuperwomanii?)

5   **CERTAIN COLORS** can make us feel certain emotions, and we can use this to our benefit. For example, this chapter is filled with images that have a yellow background, because yellow is said to evoke feelings of happiness and brightness—perfect for being a unicorn. Research colors when deciding on paint for your office or bedroom, your new notebook, or even the shirt you wear today.

Aside from minor things like towels (although, to be honest, they're pretty major), sometimes you have to make bigger decisions in life to create a better environment for yourself. Moving from my hometown, Toronto, to a new place like L.A. was really terrifying, but I knew I had to do it for my personal and professional growth. You see, in Toronto I was always the busiest person in the bunch and no one really understood my career, not even my accountant! Trying to explain YouTube views during tax season was a lot of fun. I'm pretty sure he put my occupation as "owner of the Internet." Although, I mean, heyyyyyyyy. Moving to L.A. put me in an environment where I constantly felt motivated to do more because everyone around me was blazing their own trail. In L.A., I'm surrounded by like-minded people who understand my career and I feed off their creative energy. The lack of frostbite and abundance of Chipotle locations are also huge pluses.

It is your job, solely yours, to create the best possible environment for yourself. It's not your parents' job, your boyfriend's job, or your teacher's job. It's your life, your goals, your ambitions, and therefore your task. You are a product of your environment, so decide wisely what kind of factory you want to be built in.

And, most importantly, make sure you have colorful towels.

CHAPTER 43

DON'T TALK CRAP

YOUR BRAIN

is a sponge. A massive, extra-absorbent, weird-looking wrinkly sponge that you occasionally stab with a cotton swab. It takes in the information around you whether you want it to or not. It's hungry for knowledge and stimulation, and so it gobbles up everything in sight, kind of like me at Chipotle. When we watch a movie, we're feeding our brain a story depicted in visuals being acted out on a screen. When we read a book, we're feeding our brain a story and allowing it to create its own visuals. When we meet new people, we feed our brains a new face, voice, and set of characteristics. And you know what they say: you are what you eat. So when you talk crap about people, guess what you're feeding your brain? A nice big plate of crap with no fries on the side.

Isn't it such a shame that we have this amazing piece of machinery inside our skulls that is capable of so many amazing things, but we often use it to gossip about other people? Thomas Edison's brain invented the lightbulb, and so I find it disrespectful when we use our brains to talk about how we dislike what the Kardashians are wearing. What a waste of a miracle.

A Bawse recognizes the beautiful gift of the brain and doesn't want to hurt it by feeding it junk. If you want to make a muscle stronger, what do you do? You work it. The brain is no different. Gossip has your brain sitting on the sofa drinking a six-pack of beer. You need to get it to do some jumping jacks.

My friend Humble and I recently decided that we're going to spend twenty minutes each day discussing ideas. Ideas about everything and anything are allowed. Our conversations range from inventions we believe should exist to religion and the environment. I remember having my mind blown several times during each conversation because our opinions and ideas were so different and I was learning so many new things. For example, I said, "What do you think we can do to further save the planet?" and he replied, "I think it's arrogant to think we can save a planet that gave life to us." KA-BOOM! WHAT?! I've never even thought of that. This is amazing. My mind is racing with new ideas. What if . . . ? How come . . . ? BUT! This is so much better than talking about how "stupid" or "ugly" someone is.

Sometimes you "just can't help it," though, right? We all have the natural urge to talk ill about people we dislike, mostly because in some deranged way it makes us feel better. Training your brain to think differently takes a lot of work, so instead of trying to go from gossip queen to Einstein, first try to resist the urge to infuse negativity into your conversations. Here's a challenge for you: the next time you're tempted to say something mean about someone, bite your tongue, pause, and count to ten in your head. Pretend this negative thought is your little secret that you're not going to tell anyone or release into the universe. How exciting! You have a secret that no one else knows. What power! Then, whenever you have a chance and are alone, whisper the negative thought to yourself (make sure you're alone! or else this could turn into a dramatic rom-com movie scene).

Once you master this skill, the next step is to stop allowing judgmental, mean thoughts to occupy space in your brain in the first place. When you meet someone new, instantly look at them and pick a feature to admire, and then store that in your mental contact list. If you're lucky enough to have a conversation with this person, pick a personality trait, such as calm, funny, or well-spoken. Pretend that this is a mandatory part of the process of meeting new people. Not doing so is like saving someone's number with one digit missing. Now, I know this might seem naive, but that's just because we're not used to this kind of thinking. Like most things in this book, accomplishing this will require some rewiring, so get out those pliers. Try this: Type the word "faces" into Google and click on "Images." Practice identifying one positive thing in each face. This may seem superficial, but it helps rewire our brain.

At this point you might be wondering, "If my brain should be thinking about ideas and not people, why is it okay for me to talk about people positively? Isn't that still a waste of my brain? After all, positive judging is still judging, isn't it?" Well, my intelligent friend, you're correct. Discussing all the things you like about people is still talking about people. However, if you pay attention to your past conversations, you will notice that when you talk about someone positively, you talk with a sense of admiration.

You've noticed some great quality in someone, and chances are you will be inspired to also possess this great quality. Maybe at dinner your friend was talking about all the work they've done helping less fortunate communities. If you like everything your friend is doing, then you'll probably start thinking more about getting involved yourself. It's unlikely you will admire a quality in someone and then make an effort NOT to also possess that quality.

On the other hand, when you talk about how much you hate someone's personality, you'll notice that the conversation usually lasts a really long time and is repetitive. We have the tendency to chew on that topic over and over again, and that doesn't make any sense. Is it right to spend more time on the things we don't like? Probably not. That's why, if you're going to talk about people, it only makes sense to talk about the things you like and want to incorporate into your own life.

The goal is to train your brain to think positively. Once all the positives cancel out all the negatives, there will be more space in your brain for magical creations.

IDEAS are beautiful. You can think of whatever you want without any limits. Almost everything else in life has limits, but your mind is the one thing that has no limits. So, what are you going to think about? What are you going to talk about? Are you going to waste your mind on gossip and drama? You shouldn't, because your brain deserves better. Evolution deserves better.

Spend time each day thinking about IDEAS to grow your mind and resist the urge to talk negatively about people. Your wiring is not basic, and you shouldn't be either.

"

YOUR
WIRING
IS NOT BASIC,
AND YOU
SHOULDN'T
BE EITHER.

"

CHAPTER 44

YOU'RE NOT THE

BIGGEST

BAWSE

YOU COULD BE

the richest person in the world, with forty-two cars and fourteen mansions. You could be on top of so many ladders that your home address is listed as "top rung." You could be an expert in self-control and the nicest person on the planet, with the greatest hair anyone has ever seen. In fact, you could master all fifty chapters in this book and have them memorized word for word, with a list of additional chapters I forgot to include. Even after all that, you still wouldn't be the world's biggest Bawse.

A true Bawse recognizes that there is a force more powerful than them, whether it's God, another high being, science, spirits, superpowers, evolution, or miracles. This is important for so many reasons, and understanding this chapter will help you to put into practice other lessons you may have learned throughout this book.

You know that being a Bawse entails climbing a ladder, or several ladders. When you reach the top, it's important to recognize that you're never truly at the top. There will always be a higher power that can throw you off the ladder at any time. If you believe in God, then you could be punished for your sins. If you believe in science, then you could evaporate. If you believe in spirits, then you could be possessed. If you believe in fate, then you could be struck by lightning. Knowing that there will always be a bigger Bawse one rung above you is a great way to keep yourself grounded, no matter how high you climb. This is especially important to keep in mind if you're at a place in your life where people are treating you differently because of your success. It's easy to get caught up in all the praise. You will begin to think you're untouchable, but believing in a higher power keeps your ego in check.

You can work as hard as you want to work and pull as many all-nighters as humanly possible, but without a greater force, you wouldn't have what you have. When you recognize that everything you have is because of something more powerful than yourself, you realize that it could all be taken away at any moment. That helps you appreciate what you have while you have it.

A Bawse can't control everything; they know they can control only what is within their power. Knowing that there is a higher power that controls things you cannot (weather, natural disasters, disease, miracles, etc.) is a reminder to (a) not try to control what you can't and (b) be ready to adapt to situations you have no control over. Be ready to roll with the punches that a higher power could throw your way.

I believe in God. I mean, I believe in science and spirits as well (*Paranormal Activity* has me sold), but my main higher power is God. Believing in God not only makes me feel empowered and safe but also helps me keep things in perspective. I believe that everything I have is the result of my hard work, dedication, and perseverance, but first and foremost, I know everything I have is through the grace of God. When my blessings reached God's doorstep, God signed off on the permission slip, and for that I am grateful.

Let's give it up for the higher power. You da real MVP and the biggest Bawse there ever will be.

> " THERE WILL ALWAYS BE A **HIGHER POWER** THAT CAN THROW YOU **OFF THE LADDER** AT ANY TIME.

CHAPTER 45

NO IGGYBACKS

‹- - - - - - - - - - - - - - - - - -›

YOU KNOW WHICH PICTURE

I love? The one where there's a couple or group of friends and they're giving each other piggyback rides. Everyone is laughing and pretending to be candid even though they clearly know there is a camera capturing them. Why else would they be on each other's backs like that? No one goes to the mall and decides, "You know what? I'm just going to latch on to your spine. Yup, no need for Uber—I'll just wrap around your brain stem and we'll be on our way." It's absolutely ridiculous.

I do it all the time.

Piggyback rides are cute in pictures but not in real life. It's important to know the difference between supporting people and giving them a free ride. Supporting people means encouraging them, providing them with advice, and maybe even giving them a boost to start. But it doesn't mean that you let them work less hard. Giving people a free ride means you're giving them the fruits of your labor without them having to work for it. That's like buying a broke person a Ferrari and then expecting them to pay for insurance and maintenance. My friend once scratched a Ferrari. He sleeps on my couch now.

I deal with a lot of piggyback requests. After my appearance on *The Tonight Show Starring Jimmy Fallon,* I wasn't shocked to find my Facebook inbox full of random messages. The same happened after I posted a picture with Drake. If I was elected to be a guardian of the galaxy right now, the only thing louder than the celebration party would be the notifications in my Facebook inbox. They all start the same way: "Hey! Remember me?" I do remember you. I also know why you suddenly remember me.

Side note: When you hit a certain level of success, a lot of people from your past will convince themselves that they've always supported you. Maybe they have, but they just never communicated it to you. Or showed you. Or did anything, really. But now that you're doing well, they feel some type of entitled pride and ownership.

After "Remember me?" we arrive at "So I was wondering . . . : *Can you share my video? Can you donate to my organization? Can you give my sister a shout-out? Can you attend this event? For free? And arrive with a check so you can donate to my organization? Did I already ask that?"* The most unproductive thing to do in this situation is to get upset. Of course it's a bit annoying to have people hound you for favors, especially when the last time you spoke to them was ten years ago. But that's the name of the game. These people may not even realize that I have ten other messages from ten other people that are all the same. Therefore, rather than get angry, I simply choose not to give anyone a piggyback ride. I make this very clear to people because I think it's fair and necessary for people to work hard to achieve their goals, just like I did. In fact, it doesn't make any sense for me to give anyone a free ride because they wouldn't get very far. Allow me to explain.

I have no problem supporting people who work hard and have ambition because I trust they will get far with my support. In fact, it makes me very happy to support people who I believe deserve it. As long as the effort I spend supporting someone doesn't go to waste, I have no issues. If you're creating weekly videos and putting thought into each of them but can't seem to get any views, I might share them. If you've written three quality books and really want to make the fourth one a bestseller, I probably won't mind giving it a shout-out. If you ask me for advice and I explain all the ways you can improve your channel and the next day you implement those methods, I will continue giving you advice. However, if I return to your channel one week from now and nothing has changed, I won't be encouraged to give you more advice. In the same vein, I won't share your video if you haven't made one of your "weekly" videos in two months. Why? Because it won't do anything to help you. That one video may get lots of views, and then what? If you don't put in the work to create content, my support will do nothing beyond giving your flat line a bump.

True success is built upon a strong foundation. If someone wants to use you as their escalator to success, they won't build themselves a solid foundation (refer to the chapter Take the Stairs). It's really difficult to say no to people sometimes, especially when you feel obligated to help them. My family and friends all know that I will support them but never give them a free ride (with the exception of my parents, who gave me a free ride for most of my life—shout-outs for teaching me how to walk and stuff). It's painful to do sometimes, but necessary for everyone's growth. As a Bawse, you can carry only so much weight up the ladder you're climbing. The last

"

PIGGYBACK RIDES ARE CUTE **IN PICTURES BUT NOT IN** REAL LIFE. **IT'S IMPORTANT TO KNOW THE** DIFFERENCE **BETWEEN SUPPORTING PEOPLE AND GIVING THEM A** FREE RIDE.

"

thing you want is someone relying on you for a ride and slowing down your progress. I struggle to walk up the stairs after a plate of pasta, so I don't know how I would climb a ladder with another body on my back.

Everything you encounter on your journey to becoming a Bawse is essential for you to succeed. Every all-nighter, financial investment, and milestone reached help shape who you are. In the same way, another Bawse-in-training needs to encounter the same obstacles, lessons, and sharp turns in the road. A Bawse should respect the art of hustling and make sure it doesn't become extinct. If everyone who worked hard gave all the slackers a handout, the art of the hustle would die. Support those who work hard. The hustle depends on it.

Real Recognizes Real

List three people in your life that you believe should be supported because of their hard work and determination.

1. _____

_____

2. _____

_____

3. _____

_____

Now think of specific ways you can help them.

CHAPTER 46

HAVE
VALUES,
NOT
HOBBIES

THERE ARE BILLIONS

of people on the planet. Some of those people will be pleasant and hold the door for you. Others will take your parking spot and key your car. Some people will borrow your phone charger and promise to give it back but slip it into their backpack anyway. You may encounter people who say horrible things to you, on a rainy day, when you're late for work, wearing a suit that is too small for you and drinking a coffee that contains too much milk AND you're lactose intolerant. And throughout this entire experience, your values are being tested and attacked. Thus they must be strong, because values don't get to take vacations. If you stay true to your values only when things are going well, then those aren't values; they're hobbies.

A Bawse knows that values need to be upheld even during the most difficult and stressful situations. If you get in a fight with someone who makes a racial slur toward you, is it right to respond with your own racial slur? They did it first. But does that make it right? Does that action align with your values? It is so tempting to throw our values out the window when someone pushes our buttons, but our beliefs shouldn't falter in heated situations. We're all guilty of it. We get angry and say things we don't mean, or we convince ourselves that our actions are justified.

The most universal example of this phenomenon is bullying. I'd like to believe that the average human being is against bullying. Although we've all been both victim and offender at some point in our lives, most people will tell you that bullying is wrong. We participate in anti-bullying events, use hashtags on Twitter, and support programs in schools that help students understand the effects of bullying. When we watch movies about people who are bullied, we feel for them and possibly even shed a tear. On days set aside to highlight bullying prevention, we wear a certain color to show our solidarity with the cause. Then, after all our exhausting work fighting for the cause, we get home, scroll through Facebook, and repost a video of a Kardashian having an outfit malfunction and falling flat on her face because we think it's hilarious. If that's the case, on your resume, underneath the heading that says "Hobbies," you should write "bullying."

Bullying is still bullying even if the victim is a famous millionaire. There is no justification for thinking it's okay to make fun of a celebrity. A list of justifications I often hear people use include:

- They don't have problems—they're rich.
- They'll never see it.
- They are horrible and deserve it.

Let's explore why none of these justifications are valid.

They don't have problems—they're rich. People's problems are still their problems even if they differ from yours. Let's say that, somehow, a celebrity doesn't have any problems (which, again, is next to impossible). Does that make it okay for you to bully them? Do you only believe that bullying is wrong in certain cases? Are all the seemingly problem-free people in this world fair game? Your value system should not change just because of circumstances.

They'll never see it. If you stay true to your values in public and then ditch them when no one is looking, then you don't have values, you have showpieces. If you actually believe bullying is wrong, then it doesn't matter if you are in a crowded room or stranded on an island alone like Tom Hanks in *Cast Away*. Your behavior shouldn't change.

Also, for what it's worth, many celebrities do see what's posted on social media. And even if they don't, everyone else with access to your timeline sees your behavior, and you are therefore perpetuating the belief that it is okay to bully people.

They are horrible and deserve it. Chances are you don't know the celebrity in question and you are basing your judgment of them from what you see in the media. Maybe they do or say certain things that you don't agree with, but does that make it okay to throw your values out the window? Bottom line: it doesn't matter if you deem someone to be a good or bad person, bullying is wrong.

At the end of the day, fewer people will care if you bully a Kardashian than if you bully a co-worker. But that doesn't matter. Even if other people don't hold you accountable, you should hold yourself accountable. You're a Bawse, and weak values are not in your recipe for success. When the world tempts you to go against your values, you need a shield of resistance.

Here are two ways to take your values to the gym:

1 PERSONAL MANIFESTO

When I'm having a hard time staying true to my values, I can liter-ally feel it in my soul. I can feel that I'm doing things I don't believe in, and I feel messy and dirty inside. This happens from time to time, and that's okay as long as you make an active effort to correct your behavior. And like anytime you're lost, the only way out is through clear direction. Be clear about what exactly your values are.

Years ago, I created a manifesto that outlined all the values I wanted to practice in my life. I wrote down a list of phrases, rules, and examples I wanted to live by. The list included complicated ideas that I was just beginning to understand, as well as simpler concepts that I believed were common sense. No matter how basic or how complex the value was, it went on the list. I kept adding to the list every time I thought of something new. It was like my private checklist for being a good human. Examples:

- Even if someone else is talking ill about someone, don't join in.
- Stop interrupting people and give them a chance to speak.
- Your parents were patient with you when you were younger, so be patient with them now that they're older.

Reviewing this list from time to time has been really helpful, espe-cially during those moments when I've felt like I was losing myself. I would read over the guidelines and remind myself of the person I wanted to be. It was added work, but by now you should be well aware that being a Bawse isn't easy. If you want to be a lawyer, you go to law school. If you want to be a singer, you take singing classes. If you want to be a good person with strong values, you work at it. Everything takes effort.

2 RECITE

I'm confident that every person on the planet who has graduated from the eighth grade knows two things: (1) when you don't have your hand up, the teacher will call on you anyway, and (2) the mitochondria are the powerhouse of the cell. I have literally forgotten everything else I learned in school (I think there was a dude named Freud or something, but I'm not sure; it could have been Fred) except for the mitochondria being the powerhouse of the cell. Why? Because it was drilled into my brain. In every textbook, regardless of the grade, the mitochondria were explained in the exact same way every time. I read it on the chalkboard, wrote it on tests, and said it in presentations. We should treat our values the same way we treat the mitochondria: we must ensure that we never forget what they mean. How? Study them.

Now that you've created a manifesto, you should read it once a week. Recite your values to yourself throughout the day. Doodle your values on the front of your binder. When you're upset, take a moment and visualize your manifesto. Remember who you want to be. When I need a reminder, I will often sit down somewhere alone, light a candle, close my eyes, and recite my values to myself. I want my value system to dictate my actions, and therefore it's important that I know this system well.

At the end of the day, having strong values is optional, not mandatory. There are many people out there who do not have strong values, and their beliefs change more times than a Transformer. But you, you're a Bawse, and when you believe something, it doesn't matter if it's sunny or stormy outside—you act in accordance with what you believe. Not only do strong values make you a more trustworthy and reliable person, but they help build your self-control.

Remember all those pointless math problems you had to solve in math class? Well, unlike those, figuring out your values actually matters. You're not trying to solve for the value of x or y; instead, you're trying to solve for a meaningful life.

Let your values be the powerhouse of the cell. Ha! Take that, mitochondria.

Start Your Manifesto

List three values/qualities that you hold dear to your heart and that define the type of person you want to be.

1. _____

2. _____

3. _____

CHAPTER 47

BE

NICE

TO PEOPLE

WORK HARD AND BE NICE

to people. That's my answer when people ask me what I think the keys to success are. When people hear "work hard," they usually respond with a solid head nod because obviously that makes sense. But when they hear "be nice to people," they tend to tune me out. Is being nice really necessary when it comes to success? Does it even make a difference? After all, the world isn't made up of fairies and pixie dust; it's made up of cold hard facts. Successful people are the ones who are talented, work hard, and get things done.

Well, first of all, the world has a high percentage of fairies and pixie dust, so watch your language. And second of all, if you want to talk about cold hard facts, let me give you three reasons why it's essential to be nice to people if you want to be a successful person.

66 NOT BEING NICE IS LIKE POISONING YOURSELF WITH BAD VIBES.

1 **I CAN ASSURE YOU** that every successful person you idolize has a team working behind them that they communicate with on a daily basis. Teamwork is a major ingredient in the recipe for success. Each member of the team recognizes that something larger than them is being created and that the whole is greater than the sum of its parts. You might be thinking, "I don't have a team, so this advice doesn't apply to me." But I want to remind you that you are a part of the human race, and humanity is the biggest and most important team you'll ever be on. When you start being an awesome member of Team Humanity, it'll help you be an awesome member of Team You. It's almost as though helping out Team Humanity by being nice is training for all other teams in your life. Also, minor detail, but if everyone on the planet is horrible and we all end up killing each other, you won't get the chance to become successful because you'll be dead. So there's that.

2 **SUCCESSFUL PEOPLE** understand the importance of positivity. They know that their ideas will be rejected, things will go wrong, and mistakes will be made, no matter what, and they still need to maintain a positive outlook. Have you ever met a mean person who was positive? I haven't. That's because people who aren't nice exude negative energy. When you're nice to people, you take control of the energy surrounding you. You are creating a positive environment that will help you be successful (and happy). Not being nice is like poisoning yourself with bad vibes.

3 **IN MOST SITUATIONS IN LIFE, PEOPLE** will provide you with opportunities. A person will interview you, hire you, give you a chance, sponsor you, give you a second chance, help you, teach you, and build you up. A PERSON does all of those things; therefore, it makes a lot of sense to be nice to PEOPLE. I don't see R2D2 rolling up to anyone and offering them a job, yet we probably treat our iPhones better than we do some of the people in our lives. So if being nice doesn't innately make you feel good or you don't care about humanity, realize that even for the most selfish hustler, being nice to people is essential when it comes to receiving opportunities. People will seldom work with someone who is horrible to be around.

The power of being nice to people should not be underestimated. I'm happy to say that I've established many connections and have been given many opportunities simply because I've been kind to people. Earlier this year I attended a YouTube music party and spotted Scooter Braun, aka Justin Bieber's manager, standing two feet away from me. I had never met Scooter before, but I admired his hustle and work ethic. I wanted so badly to start a conversation, but I was a little nervous and my mind was drawing blanks. I had no idea how to initiate an introduction. Should I talk about the party? Should I ask him about Justin? Should I start a formal debate about wearing socks with sandals? Should I pretend to be confused and call him Nick? After a moment of deliberation, I stopped being crazy and decided I would just tell him the truth. I walked up to Scooter and said, "Hey! I think you're really awesome, and here's why . . ."

It turns out that Scooter was having a bad day and my words really hit home. He seemed genuinely appreciative of the fact that I approached him just to say something kind. The next day Scooter posted a pic of our meeting on Instagram with a caption that read:

scooterbraun   Follow

37.8k likes   28w

scooterbraun Every once in a while someone you have never met walks up and says something to you that just makes your day. Thank you @iisuperwomanii you are awesome. Pleasure meeting you as well :)

Tell me again how being nice to people doesn't really make a difference. Since our meeting, Scooter has occasionally posted about my videos, and it warms my heart knowing that this support was birthed from a simple, kind gesture.

Being nice to people definitely includes being polite, smiling, and giving your friend the last piece of cake, but if you want to be nice like a Bawse, then you need to understand that sometimes your kindness must be proactive. This means actively thinking of ways to be nice to people that will leave a lasting impression. You should treat niceness like a task on your daily to-do list and give it as much importance as everything else.

I'd like to think that I have a reputation for being pleasant while on set. When I was doing the photo shoot for my YouTube marketing campaign, I tried my best to be super-friendly to the entire crew. This meant being patient, saying please and thank you, talking to everyone, smiling lots, having a positive attitude, and not being fussy. In my opinion, these are qualities that everyone should possess when in a similar situation. But a Bawse doesn't stop there. After the shoot I asked one of my contacts at YouTube to set up an email thread that included everyone who worked on the shoot, and I sent out an email to the entire team thanking them for their hard work and letting them know that I really appreciated their efforts and contributions. I received a ton of replies that were filled with gratitude. In fact, a few weeks later I ran into one of the directors, and he told me that no one had ever sent an email like that and it really made an impact on the team. Like a Bawse.

Before I perform, I always say the same thing to myself: "People won't always remember what you did or what you said, but they'll always remember how you made them feel." With that in mind, I go onstage and make it my goal to impact people in a positive way. This truth applies in situations beyond the stage. If you are nice to people, you will make them feel good. And when you make someone feel good, they will associate you with these good feelings. That connection is really important if you want to be successful. After all, people will want to work with, give opportunities to, and support people who make them feel good. Why would they voluntarily want to be around people who make them feel horrible? They aren't Meg and this isn't *Family Guy*. Think about it: the people you support in life are likely the people who make you feel magical inside.

Like fairies spreading pixie dust.

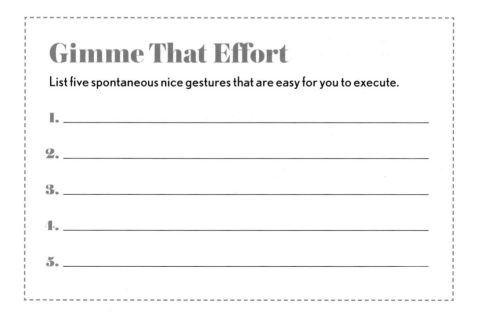

Gimme That Effort

List five spontaneous nice gestures that are easy for you to execute.

1. _____

2. _____

3. _____

4. _____

5. _____

CHAPTER 48

PROMOTE
WHAT YOU
LOVE

<-------------------->

YOUR HANDS ARE GRIPPED

around a bat. You roll your shoulders back and forth and get ready to swing with all your power. In front of you is a piñata filled with all the things you dislike: ignorant comments, ridiculous trending topics, and animal cruelty. The piñata is in the shape of a cow, which further triggers you. You take a deep breath, pull the bat back, and swing it forward with all your strength, causing the piñata to explode into pieces. Everything you hate is scattered all over the floor, and in a complete rage you continue to break those pieces into even smaller pieces. The pieces are turning into a puree at this point. You're breaking the tiles on the floor. The neighbors are complaining. Finally you stand up straight and look at all the terrible things you've bashed. You feel great . . .

. . . until the next morning, you wake up to a world filled with ignorant comments and animal cruelty. Not to mention that "Replace famous movie titles with 'butthole' " is the number one worldwide trend on twitter. How is this possible?! That's because bashing on what you hate doesn't actually get rid of it; it usually just makes you feel better for a short amount of time. If you want to solve problems, don't lash out at all the things that are wrong. Instead, promote all the wonderful solutions. In other words, promote what you love; don't bash what you hate.

> 66 PROMOTING WHAT YOU LOVE RESULTS IN SEEING MORE OF WHAT YOU LOVE IN THE WORLD.

I learned this lesson when I started doing media interviews more frequently. Prior to my appearance on *The Tonight Show Starring Jimmy Fallon,* I went through media training. One of the main lessons I learned during my training is that the media is always looking for a sound bite. More often than not, they will look for something dramatic or negative that mildly skews what you've actually intended to say. It's a sad reality, but unfortunately it's what sells in today's society. Still, I've had to learn how to handle situations in which I'm asked controversial questions, and my experiences have led me to create this mantra: promote what you love, don't bash what you hate.

Here is an example of how to apply this:

QUESTION:

What do you think about the Taylor Swift/Katy Perry drama?

ANSWER:

I think Taylor and Katy are both strong, influential women who do a lot to inspire young girls and I respect that. I think the great work they do to motivate people is more important than anything else going on.

Instead of talking about all the reasons I hate this question, I highlight everything I love about the two women I've been asked about. I want more motivational, strong women in the world, and so I'll promote that part of the story, rather than bash all the things I dislike about the media.

Imagine that your actions in real life function similarly to the way YouTube recommends videos for you to watch. The more cat videos you enjoy and watch, the more cat videos YouTube will recommend for you to watch. Positively reinforcing what you like results in more of what you like. Just the same, if you watch an abundance of gruesome murder videos, you'll be exposed to more gruesome murder videos. If you're scrolling through Facebook and see that one of your friends (aka someone you apparently went to school with ten years ago and who you barely remember) has written something you think is in bad taste, replying to the comment will probably encourage them to reply back to you, thus creating more of the conversation you disliked in the first place. Whereas if you ignored that comment and instead gave a thumbs-up to some wonderful status your sister wrote, you would continue to see your sister's post on your timeline. Promoting what you love results in seeing more of what you love in the world.

Now, it's true that there can be several exceptions to this rule. How can you not bash what you hate if someone is doing or saying hurtful things or possibly even harming something you love? We all hold certain things close to our hearts, and when they are attacked, we become triggered.

That's completely normal and expected because, surprise, we're all human. Sometimes we have to speak up about the things we disagree with. Still, with that said, it's important to recognize the difference between bashing what you hate and coming up with a solution. It's never fruitful to simply hate on something; you also have to try to fix it.

Sexism is something that really gets my blood boiling. I get sexist comments all the time, and I've gotten quite used to ignoring them. I instead focus on the positive people who support me. However, after I uploaded my video titled "Why I'm NOT in a Relationship" I received a gang of disapproving comments because people were not interested in a female declaring why she didn't need a boyfriend. A majority of the comments were from men claiming something was wrong with me. Now, I have countless videos about flirting, crushes, boyfriends, and cutesy stuff, and they're all popular. Therefore, it irked me that the one time I made a statement about being completely content without a relationship or boyfriend, I was told I was out of line. I ended up going against my self-imposed rule and replied to the comments underneath my video, highlighting how sexist they were. But does a sassy response solve the problem of sexism? No, not even if my responses were witty and completely genius, not to mention absolutely grammatically correct (a rarity on the Internet!). In addition to my sassy comments, I also made sure to highlight other comments that were in support of strong, independent women. I made reference to my social campaign #GirlLove, which aims to empower women. Furthermore, I wrote a lengthy blog post on my Facebook page encouraging people to think more critically before giving in to a sexist mindset. If I was going to let my passion get the best of me, then I had better use that passion to also promote what I love.

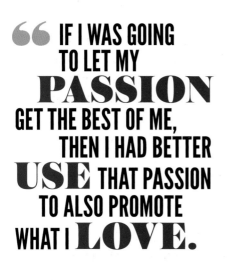

> IF I WAS GOING TO LET MY **PASSION** GET THE BEST OF ME, THEN I HAD BETTER **USE** THAT PASSION TO ALSO PROMOTE WHAT I **LOVE.**

It's all about choosing your battles and fighting those battles with tact. If you're an animal rights activist and believe everyone should be vegan, don't write a horrible comment underneath someone's Instagram picture of a McChicken sandwich. Instead, post an informative picture on your

Instagram teaching people about all the great vegan options that exist. If you believe we need to be sending more aid to remote villages in India, don't bash your friend for buying a new Mercedes; tell them about all the ways you've helped those in need and encourage them to do the same. If the option exists to promote what you love instead of bash what you don't, you should take it. And if your passion gets the best of you and you feel the need to disapprove of something, understand that mean words, hurtful jabs, and lots of exclamation marks won't solve the problem. If you're going to respond or address something you don't like, reply with ideas and words that will direct people toward the solution you love. After all, you cannot control all the things you dislike on the planet; the best you can do is inject more of what you do love into the atmosphere.

Having said all that, I'd like to send major love to all the men and women who bought this book and didn't feel some type of way taking advice from a South Asian female. I appreciate you seeing me for my intellect and not solely for my skin color or sex. Although let's be real: my skin color and sex are pretty awesome.

Lastly, no actual piñatas were hurt in the writing of this chapter.

Preach

Think of one thing you are extremely passionate about and would love to promote to the world. List three ways to do this effectively without bashing anyone.

1. _____

_____

2. _____

_____

3. _____

_____

THE
BIGGER
PICTURE

CHAPTER 49

APPRECIATE THINGS

WE'VE ALL HAD MOMENTS

when we're annoyed at the lack of perfection in our lives or when something doesn't meet our standards.

Maybe your favorite band is playing a concert and tickets are sold out. You failed your recent math test. You planned a family BBQ and it rained. You saw a brown woman on this book cover and you picked it up thinking I was Mindy Kaling and now you're utterly disappointed. YOUR LIFE SUCKS.

But here's the thing: it doesn't. Your life is actually pretty effing awesome, and a real Bawse not only recognizes this but understands how important it is to be grateful and appreciate things.

Right now you might be thinking, "Listen, Mindy imposter, you know nothing about my life, so how can you tell me it's awesome?" And to you I say, "Your life is a giant photo album and one sucky situation is simply a 4×6." Even two or three 4×6s don't make an entire album.

Let's zoom out for a minute. I know your life is awesome because you're sitting somewhere, probably in a house or a school, reading this book, which either you bought with your own money or was given to you as a gift. You're wearing clothes on your body (or maybe not, in which case, *me-ow*) and you're probably not starving. I'm going to also take a guess and say you took a shower today and tonight you will sleep in a bed. You may think this is all regular stuff, but don't make the mistake of assuming that everything you have is dismissible just because you've gotten used to it. If you're going to rate your life, rate the entire thing and don't be selective.

But I get it—you're human, and humans get used to things. We get used to the clothes we own, the water we drink, and the clean air we breathe. We forget about our privilege, and in my opinion, that is one of our biggest weaknesses. To be a Bawse, you must constantly remind yourself of all that you have to be grateful for and learn to truly appreciate those things. To do this, you need to rewire your brain. Here are a few ways to go about it:

1 One of the ways that I've been teaching myself to be more grateful is to **CALL OUT ALL THE SIMPLE THINGS** I usually overlook, saying them out loud. For example, if I'm annoyed about being stuck in traffic, I'll say, "I'm driving in a car in a beautiful city on a hot summer day." This sentence prompts me to realize that (a) I'm fortunate enough to have a car, (b) I live in a beautiful city, and (c) I'm really enjoying the weather. Then I take a good look around me and absorb the words I just spoke to myself. To make this a habit, try using this technique even when you're not annoyed or bothered by something. When I'm out with my friends having a great time, I will say "I'm having fun with my friends and we're eating a delicious dinner." When you really pay attention, there is so much to be grateful for. Right now you can say, "I'm in a safe place, reading an awesome book before I eat my lunch." DANG, you're blessed!

2 Sometimes in order to **BE GRATEFUL** you need to **WITNESS AN ALTERNATIVE WAY OF LIVING.** It's heartbreaking to say this, but it's often hard to understand how blessed you are without realizing how rough some other people have it. After all, you can't miss what you've always had. One day not long ago I was that person on an airplane very annoyed about not having Wi-Fi. I was on a fourteen-hour flight, and instead of getting work done, I had to sleep uncomfortably in a cramped space. Fast-forward twenty-four hours, and I was in the middle of Kenya. On the drive to my camp, I saw little children playing outside their huts wearing torn clothes and worn sandals. When our car drove by they ran to the road in excitement and waved to us with warm smiles. Seeing new people in a moving car was the highlight of their day. After witnessing this, I knew I could never complain about Wi-Fi ever again. Again, I get it—we all live different lives and we've come to depend on different standards of living. But sometimes it's important to put yourself in situations where you get to witness firsthand how blessed you are. You can do this by traveling, watching documentaries, reading a book, or simply viewing a YouTube video. Be aware of your privilege.

3 If you're just starting out in your career, getting into a new relationship, or beginning a new chapter in your life, it's important to **PAUSE FOR A MOMENT AND REFLECT** on what reaching this milestone means to you. It's sad to work so hard for something, only to become complacent once you've achieved your goal. Don't let your brain do that! Write yourself a letter or create a video diary reminding your future self how much your past self wanted something. For example, if you're a college graduate who's struggling to find a job and is in a really bad financial situation, write yourself a letter that outlines exactly how you feel. Talk about how much a good job would mean to you. Then, down the line, when you land that amazing job (like I know you will, because you'll work hard for it), read the letter and remember how far you've come.

I was recently talking to my friend David when he said something life-changing. He was actually repeating something his professor said to him: "There's a lot of horrible things happening in the world, and to deal with it you have two choices. You can pretend it doesn't exist and be numb to it. You can probably do this and live a long, happy life and still feel like a good person. Or you can recognize that you won the lottery with your privilege and do something with your winnings."

Being appreciative is an important ingredient in the recipe for happiness, and happiness is an important ingredient in the recipe for being a Bawse. Surprise—there's baking involved. Either you can focus on the one oddly shaped puzzle piece in your hand or you can look at the bigger picture and remember all that you are blessed with. It's your lottery money, so how are you going to spend it?

For starters, you can go out and actually buy Mindy's book. It's so damn good.

Get Grateful

List five things you take for granted.

1. _____

2. _____

3. _____

4. _____

5. _____

"

TO BE A BAWSE, YOU MUST CONSTANTLY **REMIND YOURSELF OF ALL THAT YOU HAVE TO BE** GRATEFUL **FOR AND LEARN TO** TRULY **APPRECIATE THOSE THINGS.**

"

CHAPTER 50

BE IN
SYNC

WHEN YOU THINK

of the most important team in your life, who do you think of? Maybe it's your hometown football team. Maybe it's your co-workers who all work alongside you during late nights at the office. Or maybe it's your family, the people who support you through thick and thin and know just how weird you truly are. Not the cute weird, the real weird. But while these teams are all important, none of them are as important as the team we have within us. This team governs our happiness, consciousness, and productivity.

LADIES AND GENTLEMEN! Introducing your starting lineup for the home team! Up first, weighing in at approximately three pounds, sporting a fabulous thinking cap, give it up for your MIND!

Up next, weighing five pounds more than before you ate lunch, and the only player on the team that has scored any physical points in the game, give it up for your BODY!

And last, weighing zero physical pounds but feeling like a ton, the inspiration for an entire genre of music, give it up for your SOUL!

I'll wait a moment for the crowd to settle down . . .

Conquering your mind, body, and soul and training them to work as a team allow you to align your thoughts, actions, and emotions. This alignment will not only result in genuine happiness but also provide you with the optimal conditions to be productive. After all, when a team works together, it can accomplish great things. BUT if even one member of the team doesn't cooperate, the entire team will become inefficient and disagreeable. Think of your mind, body, and soul as members of a group project. You get the best grade when everyone does an equal amount of work. As soon as one person pulls the "my computer crashed" line, the entire project suffers.

If the thought of having little team members inside yourself terrifies you, then, first of all, you need to watch *Inside Out* because this concept is actually adorable. Second of all, you can also just think of yourself as a machine. (Because robots are less terrifying than cute cartoons?! Stop it.)

Imagine you're driving your car and you turn the steering wheel left, but the wheels end up turning right. And when you step on the brakes, the car accelerates. If all the parts of a machine aren't working together, the machine will fail at performing a task. The best results come from a well-oiled machine. And that's what you should strive to make your mind, body, and soul—a well-oiled, fully functional machine that allows you to perform your best.

How can you tell if your team members are in sync? Well, is your Facebook status reflective of your actions in real life, and are those actions reflective of what you truly believe in your heart? Do you perform certain actions throughout your day that you constantly feel guilty about? Do you say you're going to do something, but then just can't get yourself to do it? If your thoughts, actions, and emotions are not all in line, then your team is not in sync. Discovering your team is not working together is an indication that you need to make some changes.

When people ask me if I'm dating anyone, I reply very honestly by saying, "No, because I'm a bad girlfriend." Chances are by the time you're reading this, nothing will have changed because artificial men don't exist and Chris Hemsworth doesn't know I exist. I discovered I was a bad girlfriend when I realized that my team wasn't in sync during my last relationship. I'd been dating my boyfriend at the time for about two years (basically, an eternity), and aside from a few incompatibilities, he was a great guy. In my mind I told myself, "He checks all the boxes, and so I definitely care about him." When people asked me about him, I would tell them the same thing. When we would argue about me not giving him enough attention or time, I would reply, "That is ridiculous. OF COURSE I CARE ABOUT YOU." Here's the thing, though: I FELT like I cared about him and I SAID that I cared about him, but I never ACTED like I cared about him. I kept prioritizing other things above him, and thus my body wasn't in sync with my mind and soul. My machine wasn't able to produce the love and dedication required for a successful relationship.

Eventually I ended things because I knew something was not right. My team didn't agree about that relationship, but it did agree about my career. Pulling an all-nighter to work on videos INSTEAD of having a conversation with my boyfriend was something all my team members agreed on. I said I would work, I felt like working, and then I worked. When I realized that my team was in alignment regarding my career, I also realized that I wasn't ready to prioritize a relationship. Basically, my mind, body, and soul were like a gold-medal-winning synchronized swimming team.

"

THINK **OF YOUR MIND, BODY, AND SOUL AS** MEMBERS **OF A GROUP PROJECT. YOU GET THE BEST** GRADE **WHEN EVERYONE DOES AN** EQUAL **AMOUNT OF WORK.**

"

Your team is there to help you make life's toughest decisions. When I was applying for graduate school, I remember THINKING I wanted to get in and ACTING like I wanted to, but my soul spoke up and got me to stop writing the essay for the application. I didn't truly FEEL good about going to graduate school, and that feeling led me to pursue my current career. Your team members will give you hints, so don't ignore them. In addition, don't ever feel like your mind, body, and soul are wrong if other people have different ideas about what you should be doing. It's your team. They play FOR YOU.

The next time you do something, pay attention to the feeling you have afterward. If you feel guilty about your actions, chances are your team is not aligned. If you regret saying something, chances are you're not in sync. If the 140 characters you type on Twitter don't reflect your character offline, you have some team building to do. It's a beautiful feeling to have your mind, body, and soul all working together to achieve a common goal. When everything is in harmony, you'll never have to lie or be fake. You can just be unapologetically yourself. Talk about #SquadGoals.

Listen to your mind. Work with your body. Feel with your soul. Be in sync. Be so N'sync that when you leave a room, you say, "Baby, bye bye bye."

Get in Sync

Think of a big decision you have coming up and answer these three questions.

What do I think I should do? _____

_____

What do I feel I should do? _____

_____

What will I actually do? _____

_____

OUT OF THE
BLUE

2007   I am nineteen years old and I've been calling myself Superwoman for years now. I'm not really sure I've earned that title, though. I think it just sounds cool and makes me feel empowered. The name helps me believe that I can get through anything, but that might just be silly of me.

I'm listening to Alicia Keys's song "Superwoman" on repeat, completely mesmerized by the music video. It features strong women who have overcome challenges and exude confidence. They deserve to be called Superwomen. No one would dispute that. I watch them with admiration, dreaming about the day when I'll be truly worthy of such a title. I want to be strong like them. I want to fight like them. I want to stand for something, like they do.

I'm inspired by the lyrics, but the feeling I have listening to the song is also bittersweet. Deep down I'm fearful that none of these words will ever apply to me. What if I'm destined for nothing great at all? What if my cape fades away and the S on my chest is just a teenage delusion? I don't know where I want to go in life or what I want to be. All I know is that I want to do something special and be known for something.

That would be a dream come true.

2016

I'm twenty-seven years old and I've been calling myself Superwoman for years now. In fact, millions of people around the world also know me by that name. Superwoman is a symbol for strength and empowerment. Young girls and boys make an S symbol with their fingers and beam with pride. I guess it makes them feel like they can get through anything.

My journey as Superwoman has taken me to a lot of cool places, but tonight I'm definitely at one of the coolest. I'm in Sicily, Italy, and we're heading to a private dinner at an ancient temple. We arrive, and it's absolutely stunning, unlike anything I've ever seen. I have a delicious meal while surrounded by amazing people and engaged in great conversation. I didn't think the night could get any better, but then it does.

Beneath the stars, I stand by the ancient ruins and listen to Alicia Keys perform live. Her voice is like food for my soul. I am captivated by her energy. I close my eyes and live the moment as thoroughly as I possibly can, feeling blessed for this opportunity. She finishes her set with power and grace, and I feel as if her performance has added years to my life.

I go back to my table and start gathering my things to leave. I'm feeling so overwhelmed that I almost don't notice the tap on my shoulder. I turn around and see the gorgeous face of Alicia Keys smiling at me. She says to me, "I was going to sing 'Superwoman' for you." A wave of emotion overcomes me. In that moment, I've officially been dubbed a Superwoman. She goes on to say how proud she is of everything I'm doing, with my book, lipstick, and #GirlLove campaign. She knows I stand for something, and those things are special.

This moment is a dream come true.

CONCLUSION

I AM SO PROUD OF YOU.

In fact, forget about me and how I feel. YOU should be so proud of yourself! You've officially graduated from Bawse training, and the world isn't going to know what hit it. I'm so hyped to see how you're going to conquer the planet, and I'll be cheering you on along the way! Take a moment and pat yourself on the back because, damn it, you deserve it. In fact, give yourself a hug and make sure you really mean it.

I truly hope that the lessons in these pages have helped you in some way. I am grateful and humbled that you've given me a piece of your time and the opportunity to share my experiences. No, really. Reading a book takes a lot of effort and patience. Thank you.

I would love to hear your thoughts on this book because it will only make me better in my own life. Below is all my social media information, so hit me up and let's have a conversation. Also, if you miss me, you can watch my videos every Monday and Thursday on YouTube. I can't promise I'll be as grammatically correct there, though. I will, however, be just as hilarious and charming.

I would like to end by saying that there is enough room in this world for all of us to succeed. We all have what it takes to be the best version of ourselves. Sometimes our inner Bawse gets knocked down and discouraged, and that's okay. That's temporary. That doesn't define you. Your strength is everlasting. You are the most powerful person in your life, and don't you ever forget that *you* call the shots.

You are a Bawse.

Keep mastering. Keep hustling. Keep making heads turn. Keep being a magical unicorn.

One love, Superwoman, that is a wrap and zoop!

WITH LOVE,

Lilly

youtube.com/user/iiSuperwomanii
Instagram: @iisuperwomanii
Facebook.com/iiSuperwomanii
Twitter: @iiSuperwomanii

ACKNOV

FIRST AND FOREMOST, I WOULD LIKE TO THANK GOD

for allowing me to live this magnificent life filled with blessings on blessings. I never need to look up and ask for your help because you've already been kind enough to give me everything I need to live a beautiful life. Thanks for the tools. Here's hoping you receive this book somehow, some way. I'll also try tweeting you.

Thank you to **MY SUPERWOMAN, MY STRONG AND BEAUTIFUL (NO, FOR REAL, SHE'S MAD HOT) MOTHER.** Just thinking about you makes me emotional, and it's literally the most annoying thing ever. WHO IS CUTTING ONIONS RIGHT NOW? STOP THAT. You have made countless sacrifices for me, even though when I was growing up I wasn't always the easiest to deal with. In fact, I was a stubborn brat. I'm sorry about that. Thank you for still loving me unconditionally. More than anything, thanks for having the guts to be a strong, epic warrior queen even in the face of adversity. **TO YOU AND DAD BOTH,** thank you for letting your crazy daughter follow her crazy Internet dreams. I know that was scary. I hope I'm making you proud. I love you.

Thank you to my **SISTER, TINA, AND HER BEAUTIFUL FAMILY,** specifically her fantastic husband and three gorgeous baby boys, for satisfying the role of good Indian daughter. Mom and Dad don't need any more grandkids, and that makes my life a lot easier. You're the real MVP.

Thank you to **MY FRIENDS,** not one of the two thousand on Facebook, but my nearest and dearest, for being my rock during some of the toughest transitions in my life. I never imagined my life would be this wild a roller coaster, and I don't know where I would be without you holding me down. Thank you, **ANOSHINIE** (babe, who are all these people?), **CHASE** (please read in your accent), **HUMBLE** (who offered me hair ties), **AMAR** (shutting down LPs since time), **SHEENA** (my favorite hippie), **NANDINI** (SPS Love), **MAATHURY** (mini Reese for life), **MAJURY** (is a great person!), and Sandy (#OOTD queen). Even to the once-upon-a-time friends I no longer speak with, thank you for shaping me and playing a role in my life. I appreciate all of you and wish you nothing but the absolute best. Truly.

Thank you to **MY AWESOME TEAM:** Sarah, Kyle, Renata, Sari, Anita, Rachel; my glam team: Ashley, Rene, and Sara; and Adryan, Kayla, and everyone at ID; Chris, TJ, Studio 71, and everyone at WME, especially my smart-as-hell literary agent, Erin Malone. She's basically a genius and probably finished reading this entire book in two hours. I know I am a crazy person, and thank you for accepting me and allowing me to destroy your inboxes on the regular.

EDGM NTS

Shout-outs to my super-cool editor, **SARA WEISS,** for helping me make sense in this book and making notes like "I don't get this joke." I really need that type of reality check from time to time. In addition, thank you to **EVERYONE AT PENGUIN RANDOM HOUSE** for being so psyched about this book. You made me feel really special and also bought me Nutella—two things I will never forget. Shout-outs to Marion Garner and Bhavna Chauhan from Canada (#WeTheNorth) and Tig Wallace and Fenella Bates from the UK.

I talk about my tour and documentary approximately 700 times in this book, and that's because it was one of the best experiences of my life. Thank you to everyone who made *A Trip to Unicorn Island* possible, including **THE ENTIRE CAST, CREW,** and **PRODUCTION COMPANY.** Let's do it again. This time, we need to address the whole "things aren't possible because of gravity" issue.

Thank you to my biggest inspirations: **DWAYNE JOHNSON, SELENA GOMEZ, JIMMY FALLON, MACHEL MONTANO, KUNAL NAYYAR, LINDSEY STIRLING,** and **ALICIA KEYS.** Writing chapters about my experiences with you both directly and indirectly has been such an honor . . . and also kind of creepy when I reflect on some particular moments. You're all really effing cool. Especially you, DJ. You've given me enough inspiration to last five lifetimes.

I'm almost done, don't worry.

Don't you dare play that soft music to force me off the stage. This is my moment.

I'd like to thank **YOUTUBE,** both the literal HTML script (or whatever) that makes the platform possible AND all the awesome people who work there for making my magical career a reality. You gave a sad girl an outlet, and I am forever grateful for your existence. To my **fellow creators,** thank you for continuously inspiring me and blazing a new, exciting path for all of us. You're the only people on the planet who can relate to the anxiety that annotations cause. I relate to you on a spiritual level. Keep killing the game!

Thank you to **#TEAMSUPER** for having my back and being the most dedicated group of Internet friends a girl could ever hope for. You support me in ways I can never understand and I love you for that. You make me smile and you make me proud.

Thank you to **ENERGY DRINKS** and **EXTRA-BUTTERY POPCORN** for being by my side throughout this entire book-writing process. I don't know where I would be without you. Just kidding. I do. I would be five pounds lighter, but that's okay. I love you for you, and you love me for me.

Also, thank you to **SPANX** for making the above note even more okay and acceptable. You literally take my breath away. You're rad as eff.

XO

PHOTO CREDITS

ABOUT

THE

AUTHOR

‹------------------------›

LILLY SINGH (AKA ііSUPERWOMANіі) is a multifaceted entertainer. She has found worldwide fame through her comedic and inspirational YouTube videos, amassing more than eleven million subscribers. She has appeared in the feature films *Ice Age: Collision Course* and *Bad Moms*, and in 2016 she starred in and produced her own feature-length film, *A Trip to Unicorn Island*. As a role model to women and girls around the globe, Singh created her #GirlLove initiative to break the cycle of girl-on-girl hate and fight for gender equality.

Singh was named to the *Forbes*'s 2016 30 Under 30: Hollywood & Entertainment and *Fast Company*'s Most Creative People in Business 2016 lists. She has made numerous television appearances, including multiple stints on *The Tonight Show Starring Jimmy Fallon* and has been featured in *Entertainment Weekly, People, Elle Canada, Seventeen, Vogue India, The Wall Street Journal*, and *The New York Times*, among others. A successful entrepreneur, Singh released her own signature lipstick, called Bawse, with Smashbox and has also partnered with Coca-Cola.